Woman Battering
as Marital Act

To Martin, Sofia and Jonas

Margareta Hydén

Woman Battering
as Marital Act

The Construction of a Violent Marriage

Scandinavian
University Press

Scandinavian University Press (Universitetsforlaget AS), 0608 Oslo
Distributed world-wide excluding Norway by
Oxford University Press, Walton Street, Oxford OX2 6DP

Oxford   New York   Toronto
Dehli   Bombay   Calcutta   Madras   Karachi
Kuala Lumpur   Singapore   Hong Kong   Tokyo
Nairobi   Dar es Salaam   Cape Town
Melbourne   Auckland   Madrid
and associated companies in Berlin   Ibadan

Oxford is a trade mark of Oxford University Press

Published in the United States
by Oxford University Press Inc., New York

© Universitetsforlaget 1994

Cover illustration:
© Christer Jonson

British Library Cataloguing in Publication Data
Data available

ISBN 82-00-21806-6

Library of Congress Cataloguing in Publication Data
Data available

Typeset by HS-Sats A/S
Printed in Norway by HS-Trykk A/S, 1994

Contents

Foreword

I am delighted to write a Foreword for this outstanding book. But let me warn the reader, it is not an easy book, not because it is poorly written or conceptually muddled, it's exceptionally logical, coherent and theoretically integrated. The book is difficult to read because of its topic and methodological approach. Margareta Hydén gained access to intimate accounts of marital violence, graphic descriptions by participants of events that are morally repugnant to all of us. Private behavior became public only because the women came forward to police and hospitals, or social authorities came forward on women's behalf. Some of the women barely escaped death. I found myself able to continue reading (and there were points when I had to put the book down) only because Margareta Hydén makes such theoretical sense of senseless acts. The book sheds light on the social organization of marriage, gender relations, Swedish society, human nature itself.

The goal of the research was to understand the social psychological process of woman battering in marriage from several perspectives: the male perpetrator, the female victim, and the couple engaged in the joint project of marriage. In the background are the children ("participatory witnesses" to their parents' violence and its "indirect victims"). Put in the terms of symbolic interaction theory, Margareta Hydén explores the various definitions of the violent situation – the woman, the man, the couple, the public authorities charged with its control. She asks how participants make sense of it and, more specifically, how understandings change over time in ways that make marriage impossible, or possible (and 50% of the couples are still together two years after her initial interviews with them). Unusual in the scholarly literature on marital violence, this book examines the natural history of a violent incident – how it is structured, sequenced, and interpreted, how it unfolds, erupts, and then is explained by participants, how the violence is integrated or dissociated from lives.

To make theoretical sense of her data, Margareta Hydén sews together a quilt that is composed of diverse squares of cloth. At the most macro level, she stitches in the work of Blumer to argue that a social problem does not exist unless it is recognized by a society. The

age-old (private) phenomenon of woman battering has only recently
been defined as a social problem, subject to control by (public) agen-
cies. The collective redefinition of private violence as a crime is to a
great extent the product of the modern feminist movement, and
Margareta Hydén describes how this happened historically in
Sweden, culminating in a change in the law in 1982. At the meso-
theoretical level, she stitches into her quilt squares from family
theory. Marriage is a form of social organization she argues, a set of
social relations between individuals (called husband and wife) that
are governed by rules, norms and expectations of how marital life
should occur. In contrast to some sociological theorizing, the emphasis here is on how the rules *constitute* action; "marriage is its
marital rules". People construct what marriage is supposed to be by
doing it in particular ways. In the context of Swedish society,
violence against the wife breaks a rule (law), yet it is, in the author's
words, a "morally *questionable* marital act". There is considerable
latitude for the couple to develop their own understandings of what
happened. Whether marriage can be constituted with violence as a
part of it depends on how a violent incident is interpreted.

Another square in the theoretical quilt comes from feminist
theory, which emphasizes the hierarchical power structure of traditional marriage. Violence is the quintessential act that displays
patriarchal power relations; men are dominant and women are
subordinate. While clearly sharing a feminist agenda, Margareta
Hydén shifts the angle of vision: "A husband's use of violence
towards his wife, and the way she reacts to it, produces a social order
(e.g. marriage) as well as *reflects* an already existing social order in
the surrounding society."

Finally, micro-level theorizing provides squares for this diverse
quilt. On the one hand, there is a theory of personal accounts: when
the untoward happens, individuals develop accounts to excuse or
justify it, as Lyman and Scott argue. This line of argument is applied
to the couples' accounts of violence in marriage. On the other hand,
Margareta Hydén brings narrative theory to bear: one way individuals make sense of the violence is by casting it into the form of
a story, with protagonists and culminating events. She makes creative
use here of Kenneth Burke's concept of dramatism. The grammatical
resources that individuals employ to tell persuasive tales are contained in the pentad of terms: Act, Scene, Agent, Agency, Purpose. She
found that both women and men used these elements to construct
their stories, but each emphasized different ones. The husband
stressed purpose, the wife stressed agency (how he did it) and the
consequences of the violence for her, physically and emotionally.

The sum of the squares, the quilt that Margareta Hydén produces from various theories about social life, is an original configuration, and sufficiently colored and textured to display her longitudinal data. The interviews were with twenty couples (conducted over a two-year period with the wife, husband, and the couple together in most cases), and she describes the experience of carrying out the interviews. Drawing on the work of Elliot Mishler, she approaches them as conversations, a discourse among speakers. All parties are active agents, teller and listener/questioner alike, with informants and investigator constructing reality together.

As she examines the narratives, Hydén finds that "his" and "her" accounts are similar in some ways and different in others. She locates a common narrative sequence, organized by time, with a beginning, middle and end. There is a pre-history, a violent incident, and an aftermath to the story. Hydén organizes her narrative about their narratives into these three phases. What was not talked about proved to be as important to her analysis as what was discussed. She deconstructs the texts, looking for gaps and inconsistencies. Her method is interpretative – totally appropriate for a study of women's and men's interpretations of experience.

Reading the results of her analysis of the narrative accounts, I was struck by several aspects. There is a typical interactional sequence in the pre-history, a "mundane" request (e.g. one speaker asks for paper towels to clean up a mess) that is denied, which then provokes a fight. There is a missing link in the sequence – how the second speaker interprets the first speaker's utterance; she "reads his request as humiliating and insulting, so denies it". Consistent with the work of sociolinguist William Labov (who studied violence between men), Margareta Hydén identifies how the status of the spouses is thrown into question by the denial of the request. She argues theoretically that by these interactional sequences, couples create a hierarchical social order, with each party trying to gain advantage over the other.

Once violence erupts, husbands and wives language their descriptions of it in strikingly different ways. He minimizes seriousness by calling it a "fight", while she maximizes it and implies the violence was one-way by calling it an "assault". Language is important because an "assault" is difficult to integrate, that is, to continue the marital relationship with violence as a component, whereas a "fight" is easier – it can be compatible with married life. Men's descriptions suggest marriage can continue, women's suggest the opposite.

Looking at the couples who remained together (50%) in the aftermath phase there is concerted work on the part of both husband and wife to neutralize the violence. Margareta Hydén insightfully analyzes how, momentarily, the gender hierarchy reverses itself: the husband becomes submissive to the wife, subjugates himself to gain absolution. Both spouses redefine what happened; what she labeled "an assault" in an earlier interview gets constructed differently during the aftermath (alcohol is blamed, for example, not the man who drank it). The net effect is that the husband is released from responsibility. But there are deep costs: a violent marriage is created, a form of social organization that can give refuge to male violence.

Feminist scholarship has tended to portray women as victims, and Hydén clearly positions her work within the feminist tradition. But she complicates the story in ways that make some feminists uncomfortable. Women participate in the construction of hierarchy in marriage, she argues, they are not only victims of it. She brings into view the contradictions of gender relations: "that which makes him strong, dangerous, and dominant (violence)...also makes him small, helpless and dependent on a wife. That which makes the woman weak, helpless and dependent (violence) is also what makes her strong in the sense of perseverance and patience." The book makes a major contribution to our understanding of violence in marriage precisely because of these adept and nuanced understandings. It is a work of exceptional interest, and bears witness to a problem that has remained hidden too long.

Catherine Kohler Riessman
Boston University

Acknowledgments

This study traces its origin from a most stimulating clinical environment, the "Nacka Project", an experiment in the provision of social psychiatric services in a community near Stockholm. As a young social worker, and later as a psychotherapist, I had the privilege of having the director, Johan Cullberg, as my tutor. Johan taught me to listen carefully to personal narratives. He made me aware of the process of interviewing as a jointly conducted discourse between the speakers. My debt to him runs very deep.

I am also very grateful to Thomas Lindstein, School of Social Work in Stockholm, for his support throughout the years. In his generous, considerate, and critical fashion, he has read version upon version of the manuscript – without evident weariness. My thanks to Stig Elofsson for statistical advice and stimulating discussions, and to Sven-Axel Månsson for his careful reading of the final version of the manuscript. My sincere thanks also to Anders Nyman for his indispensable assistance during the long period of data collection.

To Per Linell and his colleagues at the Department of Communication Studies, University of Linköping, I would like to express my thanks for helpful discussions about the structure of verbal aggression.

Crucial discussions of my study took place at the Family Research Laboratory, University of New Hampshire. I would like to thank Murray Straus and David Finkelhor especially, as well as their fellow researchers, for their constructive criticism.

The *All Women's House* in Stockholm, a meeting place for women and a shelter for battered women, headed by Cecilia Önfelt, is next on my list to be acknowledged. Few places are so filled with energy and joy. I thank all you women, and especially Cecilia, for letting me be a part of your community.

Through our endless discussions, Lars-Christer Hydén, with his extensive knowledge and sharp analytical mind, has played a central role in the "intellectual everyday life" from which this study emerged.

To Karen Leander, dear friend and first-rate translator, my sincere thanks for making this manuscript readable in English. Further thanks, Karen, for your attentive reading and your creative solutions to issues unrelated to linguistic errors.

This study owes much to a very supportive and productive research environment – a women's studies milieu in Norway, headed by Hanne Haavind at the University of Oslo. At an early stage of this work, I persuaded her to be my constant conversational partner. To say that I owe her a debt of deep gratitude would be the understatement of the year. She has shared her subtle and creative thinking with me in an overwhelmingly generous manner. She has been the careful midwife to my study.

My thanks also to the Commission for Social Research and to the University of Stockholm, who financially supported this project.

My greatest debt is to the interviewed women and men who so openly shared their experiences with me. As I have taken every precaution to preserve the anonymity of all of you, I cannot thank you publicly.

Martin, Sofia, and Jonas, my dear children, my thanks to you for patting me on the cheek at my low points.

This study at times depressed me and made me dubious about the chances for women and men to live together. My final thanks go to Lars-Christer, for letting me experience that a woman and a man are able to share a good life.

Stockholm September 1993
Margareta Hydén

1

The Social Psychological Meaning of Marital Woman Battering

The conceptualization of female experience of male violent behavior

On a winter day in February, 1863, in Stockholm, Sweden, Chief Constable Åkerdal received a visit from two women. The police records show that the younger woman, around 20 years old, spoke first:

> Unmarried Maria Theresia Grosse has related that she has been violated by her father and forced by him over a long period to carnal knowledge, to which she was pressed by means of threats and battery. (Court Reports 1874)

The older woman is then paraphrased:

> Madame Grosse corroborated her daughter's claim. The wife is 40 years old and is now pregnant; she has well been aware of these circumstances but has not dared or been able to prevent them, in part out of fear of violence and in part due to the economic difficulties to support their large family if her husband were to be incarcerated. The husband is said to be 41 years old and of a wild and treacherous nature, capable of being angered to the extreme, and to have threatened his wife's and children's lives as soon as his goings on with his daughter were exposed. (Court Reports 1874)

A month later, Maria Theresia continued her tale, now in the Stockholm District Court:

> It started when I was a child; my father used to try to cohabit with me without succeeding. Cannot remember when my father succeeded in satisfying his unnatural lust with me. As long as I stayed in my parent's home, he did not succeed. But when he obtained work in a neighboring town, he prevailed upon me to follow along as his assistant at work. We each lived in our own room. My father came several nights into my room and regardless of my resistance, he lay down beside me, uttering that it should be so that children were obedient to their parents, and then he hit me and threatened me with battery if I did not submit. So he had carnal cohabitation with me. (District Court Reports 1863)

Thus, a mother and daughter describe a series of events which they had endured over years of suffering. They tell of threats, blows, and sexual violation.

The father claims "to have been forced" to have intercourse with his daughter. He denies having struck her. Perhaps he had once grabbed her violently and pushed her down. Otherwise, he had always succeeded in persuading her. He had hit her with a cane and whip when he was jealous. He quotes from the Bible to support his statement that children have a duty to obey their parents. He had found quotations proving that he had acted properly towards his daughter. At the same time, he knows he had acted wrongly. He had threatened his wife and children with their lives if they told any other living soul about what happened in their home. He had struck his wife and their children.

In the court, the mother has difficulty giving her testimony. She is in an uneasy mental state and is several months pregnant. She appears "confused" and has "considerable difficulties to talk". Maria Theresia and her sister Ernestine Louise, on the other hand, carefully describe the violence and violations they had been subjected to.

What the court hears, though, is somewhat different from what the women say. While the women talk about physical and sexual attacks, the court's interest fastens on a single question: Has intercourse occurred between the father and one or both daughters? If so, this would indicate the commission of a criminal act – that of incest. No interest in any other acts of cruelty, by the husband and father towards his wife and daughters, is to be found in the court records.

The court established that "carnal cohabitation" had taken place between the father and one of the daughters, Maria Theresia. The father received a life sentence to hard labor. Assisted by his sons, he sought a pardon several times in the following years. In 1873, he was pardoned. By then, he had been suffering from a lung disease for many years. Prior to his pardon, Maria Theresia wrote to the prison governor:

> As it has come to my attention that my father has anew sought to be pardoned by His Royal Highness, I must beseech the Governor-Director in all humility, that in the case that his plea is granted, he must be convinced to take to another town, where he will be unable to disrupt the calm that I, my mother, and my siblings have achieved after such suffering. (Court Reports 1874)

The family then disappears from the public records for all posterity.

In this way, the fate of the Family Grosse became the subject of judicial attention in 1863 in Stockholm's District Court. From the records, there seems to be no doubt that the three women of the family had been struck. The husband and father had admitted to hitting all of the women with his fists as well as with weapons.

Nevertheless, there is nothing in the court records to indicate that the members of the court had to any tangible degree focused on the physical violence that the women had been subjected to, or threatened with. The members of the court could acknowledge the *reality* of woman battering that afflicted the Grosse women, whereas the *concept* of woman battering did not exist in the sense that it is used today. In the Sweden of 1863, the phenomenon of woman battering obviously existed, but had not been delimited, named, or described as a social phenomenon. Consequently, it was neither named nor reacted to in the public sphere as "woman battering".

In contrast, the sexual relations between the father and his daughter Maria Theresia were dealt with judicially. They were defined as actions of incest. Not least of all in Biblical teachings, such actions were long before 1863 identified and declared by Swedish law to be illegitimate. This is what made the judicial outcome in the Stockholm District Court possible.

In present day Sweden, approximately 9,500 assault cases are annually reported to the police where a woman is assaulted indoors by a person known to her (SCB 1991). These crimes are almost entirely dominated by men who assault their current or previous wives, cohabitées, or fiancées (Wikström 1987 p. 23). Studies have shown that the frequency of violence within families is substantially higher than indicated by the number reported to the police. These studies find it probable that the actual violent criminality is at the very least three times greater than the registered criminality, that is, crimes reported to the police (Wikström 1987 p. 13).

In today's Sweden, the issue of woman battering is the focus of extensive attention in the mass media and by the social welfare and health care authorities. In 1982, the rules for prosecuting assault cases were altered so that woman battering, including non-aggravated assault on private property, is subject to public prosecution in the sense that the question of whether a batterer will be prosecuted or not is no longer dependent on the victim's wishes in a formal sense. If a case does come to the attention of the police, the State becomes the accuser and not the victim. The man is to be held accountable to the State, via the judiciary. Thus, woman battering no longer formally exists solely in the private sphere. The private phenomenon has become part of the public sphere, a publicly regulated social problem.

From this point onwards, the word "assault" will be used to indicate those acts which are likely to be included in the legal concept of "assault and battery". There is no separate category in the Swedish Criminal Code for "wife battering", which is included under "assault".

The contrast between the present-day description of woman battering as a publicly regulated problem and the historical description of an obviously existing but unspeakable phenomenon, illustrates the operation of a social process: The process of definition of a certain kind of female experience, namely, that of male violent behavior towards a woman in intimate relationships.

As stated by Blumer in his article on "Social Problems as Collective Behavior", "social problems are not the result of an intrinsic malfunctioning of a society but are the result of a process of definition in which a given condition is picked out and identified as a social problem" (Blumer 1971 pp. 301-302). According to Blumer, a social problem does not exist for a society unless it is recognized by that society as existing. The process of collective definition determines the emergence of social problems, the way in which they are seen, the way in which they are approached and perceived, and the kind of official reaction they receive.

Not until quite recently did the female experience of male violent behavior become visible in a manner that has made it open to examination. In consequence, my work relies heavily on the process of social definition that turned woman battering from its status of an unspeakable reality to a conceptualized social problem.

The main concern of my work has been devoted to the study of the kind of violent actions a woman can be submitted to *within marriage,* that is, violence against a woman at the hands of her husband.

The first task of this study was the *identification and description* of the violent acts as they appeared and were committed by the man within the marital life of the spouses.

The second task was to *understand how the involved parties made sense* of the violent action, that is, how they defined and interpreted, explained, and justified it. Accordingly, my interest was mainly concentrated on the involved parties, the battering man and the battered woman, and on their understanding of what had happened. I was less interested in commentaries by those around them, including comments made by social scientists.

In order to set the stage for what follows, however, I will continue my summary of the process of definition of the concept of woman battering. This summary will include a description of the essential feature of the concept as it appears in our era and in our Western cultural context.

Woman battering in fiction

The "unspeakable" realities of human experience, those kinds of experiences that cannot appear in documentary form, in court files, or within the social sciences, have most frequently been found in fiction. Moa Martinsson is one of the Swedish writers who depicted the violence women experienced in their own homes during the early decades of the 1900s. In one of her novels, *Women and Appletrees* (1985), she describes how the main character's husband (Bernhard) had become extremely irritated with his wife. He visits his neighbor in the next cottage:

 After a few hours, Bernhard and the crofter were agreed: Women need to be hit when the locoweed gets to them. Otherwise, they stay crazy. The two men's wives had once smashed a still right in front of the crofter's eyes. Since that day, he had beaten his wife as soon as she had so much as raised her voice above the usual.
    – Don't you see Bernhard, there's nothing else to do. If your woman starts acting devilishly, just hit her. (Martinsson 1985)

According to Martinsson's narrative, the prevailing conception of woman battering in the first half of the twentieth century could probably be paraphrased as "if your husband neither abuses alcohol, nor you, you can consider yourself a lucky woman". Battering in those days was a common, unwanted reality for many women.

Merely on the basis of the fate of the Family Grosse and that of women in literature, it is impossible to draw any far-reaching conclusions about whether violence against women occurred more often in the Sweden of 1860 or in the beginning of the twentieth century than is the case today. We cannot interpret the lack of the concept "woman battering" in earlier periods as an indication of less knowledge or experience of this violence. A more feasible interpretation would be that battering in the home constituted an integral part of women's and children's lives to such a degree that it was then difficult to isolate it from other aspects of family life. The above quotation would support such an interpretation.

The social construction of woman battering in modern times

The contemporary conception of woman battering is to a great extent a product of the modern feminist movement. In American women's history, the battered woman movement is described as a "by-product" of the feminist movement of the 1970s. When women congregated in women's political and consciousness-raising groups and shared their personal experiences, it was revealed that they shared the experience of having been victimized by violence. They had previously kept this secret, since they had seen it as an individual problem, as a personal failure. Suddenly, it became an experience they had in common with other women (Studer 1984). A similar development took place in England. When the English journalist Erin Pizzey opened a women's house in Chiswick outside of London in the 1970s, her intention was to provide a meeting place for housewives in the area. Soon the house was filled with women seeking protection (Pizzey 1974).

Swedish women also formed women's political groups during the 1970s. In 1976, a meeting was arranged in Stockholm for all women who were interested in opening a women's shelter. A women's house group was formed. In 1980, *All Women's House* opened in Stockholm. Similar centers grew up around the country. Battered women emerged from their obscurity and gave witness to their experiences. The shelter workers accumulated a massive experience of the problem. They gained insight into what actions needed to be taken and what services were lacking, as well as into the inadequacies of the social welfare organization (Bolin 1989).

The material provided by the battered woman movement became first-page news in Sweden in the early 1980s. What the women told was shocking, sensational, and incredible for most people. The women's movement used the attention attracted by the exposure of woman battering to define the problem as a public problem.

As an element in the struggle to define woman battering as a public problem, a change needed to be made in the existing criminal law. Previously, for non-aggravated assault in a private place to be prosecuted, the victim's request that this be done was required. Therefore, the women's movement sought to bring assault in a private place – that is, the home – under public prosecution. The then existing legislation implied indirect support of violence in the family, since it was left to the woman to determine whether she could – or dared to – prosecute the man.

The position of the women's movement was that it was the Swedish State through its prosecutorial branch that should act as accuser and hold the man accountable, in order to demonstrate that the man's behavior was illegal. The law was changed in 1982, when all assault, regardless of where it occurs, was declared to be a matter for public prosecution.

The modern women's movement viewed woman battering as violence against women of a gender-specific type, where the man was the perpetrator and the woman the recipient of the violence. Its ultimate cause was to be found in the "patriarchal societal structure" that placed men in a dominant position in relation to women.

The women's movement analyzed woman battering as encompassing both physical and mental violence against women. The determination of what was to be considered woman battering with regard to the seriousness and setting of the violence, however, was not clearcut. Instead, it was seen as important that the woman herself determine whether or not she had been battered.

The women's movement converted its newly acquired knowledge into *political* demands for change in the power relations between the sexes, something that feminist researchers contributed to indirectly, but never agitated for directly. One such demand concerned a change in the laws for assault crimes. A further demand concerned the establishment of women's shelters, both as a protection for battered women and as a base for the continuing political efforts of the women's movement.

In my opinion, it is the women's movement's self-produced understanding of woman battering, that which was absent from the academic journals and for which there are no statistics, that has played the most dramatic role in changing the general cultural understanding of the phenomenon in Sweden and in the other Scandinavian countries. This understanding has contributed to changes in women's self-understanding, both among battered women and other women. However, there is a potential problem with the modern women's movement's unceasing emphasis on the woman's role as *victim* in the violent context. Security, protection, and exculpation from responsibility for violence – which await women at women's shelters – are not sufficient to create a change in a battered woman's life. For this, the opposite must be emphasized: her ability to act and to take responsibility for her own life.

Feminist research on woman battering

During the latter part of the 1970s and during the 1980s, the discussion and exchange of information in this field came to be dominated by feminist researchers and proponents of the modern women's movement, and not seldom in one and the same person. However, this theme has not played a central role in Swedish feminist research, which has had serious consequences both for the development of feminist theory and for the very definition of gender equality (Elman and Eduards 1991).

In international research – and I here include the much more active scholars in the neighboring country of Norway – feminist researchers argued that woman battering was an unusually clear and brutal example of vigorous patriarchy in our society and of male dominance. According to feminist researchers, the cause of woman battering is to be found in such a context and is not to be looked at from the viewpoint of individual pathology. Feminist scholars asserted that woman battering was not the expression of a psychological problem, not in the man, the woman, nor in the family.

The determinating factor of the traditional marriage, according to feminist theory, is its hierarchical power structure, with the man in the dominant and the woman in the subordinate position. In the eyes of feminists, the batterer is an oppressor, a representative of the dominant male sex, and the woman, a representative of the subordinated female sex, is his victim.

It is primarily historical data, as well as case descriptions from the modern era, that are used for analyzing the link between a "patriarchal societal" system and woman battering. One of the most well-known examples of this approach is the work of the Scottish researchers Dobash and Dobash, who put the phenomenon in a historical perspective and complement this by means of interviews with women at women's shelters. They wrote that:

> ...men who assault their wives are actually living up to cultural prescriptions that are cherished in Western Society – aggressiveness, male dominance, and female subordination – and they are using physical force as a means to enforce that dominance. (Dobash and Dobash 1979 p. 24)

In their case descriptions, these feminist researchers allowed the woman as an individual being to come forward. They made it possible for her to do so by providing her with protection – the majority of interviews took place at a shelter – and by listening to her without challenging her story. During long interviews, the researchers listened to the women who related their experiences as victims of wife battering. They took notes and analyzed these stories. The battered woman's story was identified, acknowledged, and given a name (Martin 1976; Dobash and Dobash 1979; Walker 1979; Schechter 1982; Araldsen and Clasen 1983; Christensen 1984; Skjörten 1986; Yllö and Bograd 1988).

Much of the feminist work concentrated on describing *the consequences of woman battering*. The psychologist Walker (1978) describes how the woman's personality is eventually altered, as she *learns to be helpless*. Walker also describes how battered women perceive themselves as having been *brainwashed* by their husbands, who had convinced them of their incompetence, hysteria, and frigidity. Such "brainwashing", followed by physical violence, is powerful. The family is a primary group, within which most individuals form their perception of reality and the family members often do not have sufficient contact with the outside world to compel adjustments in these perceptions. One result of this psychological manipulation of reality is a tendency for the victim to *blame herself* (Walker 1979 pp. 525–534).

Another characteristic that battered women share is an extreme feeling of *shame and humiliation,* and subsequently a feeling of alienation. Long-lasting effects on the battered woman are serious psychological symptoms such as depression, suicidal impulses, self-contempt, and an inability to trust other people or to develop close relationships (Butler 1978; Araldsen and Clasen 1983; Christensen 1984).

Substantial efforts have been devoted to attempting *to define the concept of battered wife.* In this context, Walker (1979) raises the question of *the frequency of the violence,* and maintains that a battered woman is a woman who at least two times has undergone all three phases of this type of violence:

> The battering cycle appears to have three distinct phases, which vary in both time and intensity for the same couple and between different couples. These are: the tension building phase; the explosion or acute battering incident; and the calm loving respite. (Walker 1979 p. 55)

The English psychologist Pagelow (1981) studies *the subjective experience* of violence as a dimension of the definition of a battered wife. She states that "a slap means different things to different people", and continues that it is unwise to stop at objectively identifiable actions in a definition of a battered woman. The consequences of a violent act for an individual woman are in part dependent on the objective event, but also on how it is perceived by the woman (Pagelow 1981).

The use of men's dominance and women's subordination as the cornerstone of analysis in feminist research has led to a complementing of research on woman battering and a comparison of it with research on other types of violence against women, such as rape, incest, and street violence (Russel 1982; Wardell, Gillespie and Leffler 1983; Stanko 1985).

The Norwegian theologian and feminist researcher Lundgren has studied the consequences of woman battering and the process that leads to the maintenance of the violence in a sample of women and men in 32 couple relationships from a religious milieu on Norway's west coast (Lundgren 1989). She found that a "normalization process" evolves where the man and woman each develops a strategy for achieving certain defined objectives. She called this strategy "goal-means strategy", which is initially linked to the man's notions about what a man and a woman and a good couple's relationship ought to be. The normalization process that the man undergoes was described by Lundgren as "a goal-oriented strategy for establishing control over the woman and the possibility for constituting masculinity", and the corresponding process for the woman as "a strategy for adjustment, the minimal possibility for retaining some control" (Lundgren 1989 pp. 113–140).

Feminist researchers focused on and gave a name to women's experiences. The woman as a separate human being was allowed to step forward, and the gender-specific nature of woman battering was emphasized. To focus on the gender-specific nature of the phenomenon was of decisive importance for the understanding that emerged. The feminist tradition had several points of interest in common with the women's movement and was influenced by it, not least of all in that many feminist researchers were members of the women's movement. In order to see this violence as violence, to be able to view the woman as a person, and to see the gender-specific character of this violence, required that the violence be distanced from gender-neutral descriptions such as "domestic fighting" or "spouse abuse", and terms were instead used such as "woman battering" or "wife abuse".

Individual psychological research on woman battering

Psychologists and psychiatrists are some of the most active researchers of the family. Their view of marriage is one of harmony. In their perspective, the root of what happens in the family is most often found in the personalities of the family members, and nothing that the institution of marriage could be held responsible for.

The first descriptions of woman battering – prior to those by battered women and workers in shelters – were presented by researchers and clinicians within this field.

In 1960, the probation officer Schulz wrote an article called "The Wife Assaulter" (1960). Schulz sought the cause of woman battering by means of analyzing the personality characteristics of the violent man. In the article, four men convicted of the attempted murder of their wives are described. The men's upbringing was characterized by dominating, rejecting mothers, who were largely aggressive towards them. The initial reaction of the men was submissiveness, at the same time that they identified with the mother and her aggressiveness. They were never able to channel their own aggressiveness in a normal fashion. Throughout their lives, they remained passive and yielding, rigidly checking their aggressive impulses. In their relationships to their wives, they reproduced their relationship to their mothers. They related to their wives more as mothers than as wives, and adopted a submissive position in relation to them. When the men's needs for intimacy and dependence were frustrated, their aggressiveness increased. They were constantly torn between their hostility towards their wives and their dependence on them. The aggressive outburst occurred at the point the man interpreted something as the ultimate rejection, such as the discovery of his wife's infidelity or her request for a divorce (Schultz 1960 pp. 103–112).

In Sweden, men who batter women have been classified by the psychiatrist Johan Cullberg, in his textbook *Dynamic Psychiatry* (1984, in Swedish), as falling into four groups:

1. Men who have committed *occasional "moderate/minor" assaults* or who threaten violence but who otherwise are not particularly criminalized. The battering often occurs in connection with alcohol consumption and under strong affect. Whereas the other groups are more characterized by an ego-split of a borderline nature, this group of men is closer to being an inhibited group with powerful superegos; men who in acute situations can become overwhelmed by an early repressed aggressive problem-matrix.
2. *Recurring assault/battering* of otherwise non-criminalized men with or without alcohol in the picture. These men may go around with a powerfully charged aggressive conflict that is triggered now and then. This group is perhaps the most dangerous due to the fact that they are the hardest to detect. This is related to the fact that the two sides of the man, the violent and the decent, are not outwardly compatible with each other. The correlation first becomes visible when examined according to the psychodynamic theory, that describes the ego-splitting mechanism of keeping mutually conflicting personality traits separate and hindering any confrontation between them.
3. *Sexually sadistic crimes.* These men have serious early emotional disturbances.
4. Men who commit *serious repeated violent crimes* – marginalized, criminal, alcoholic. They are often seriously mentally disordered or brain-damaged of psychopathic character. (Cullberg 1984 p. 307)

Schultz and Cullberg as well as other individual psychology-oriented researchers (Faulk 1974; Gondolf 1985; Hamberger and Hastings

aintain that battering men have certain personality traits in
on, traits that predispose them to subjecting their partners to
ce. According to these writers, the cause of woman battering is
found in the man's childhood history and in his personality
development.

Schultz's article was unique, not only because it was one of the
first written about woman battering, but also because it dealt with
the man. Over the ensuing 20 years, the general interest would shift
to the battered woman. The perpetrator of the violence became
notably absent in research on woman battering.

Four years after Schultz, three forensic psychiatrists, Snell, Rosenwald, and Robey wrote the article "The Wifebeater's Wife" (1964).
With this article, they were among the first to describe the battered
woman from an individual psychology perspective. The article was
based on a study of twelve couples in which the woman had reported
her husband for assault. The intention of these authors had initially
been to submit both the women and the men to psychiatric examinations, but it was much easier to get the women to comply with their
requests. The women were willing to present their version of the
events, whereas the men were more restrained with the psychiatrists
(Snell et al. 1964 p. 108).

Snell, Rosenwald, and Robey presented a dismal view of these
women. They described them as aggressive, efficient, masculine, and
sexually frigid. They were controlling towards the men at the same
time they were dependent on them. The men were described as
passive, indecisive, impotent, and alcoholized (Snell et al. 1964
p. 111). These three psychiatrists found the origin of woman battering
in the combination passive man/aggressive woman.

Similar reasoning is found in the work of British psychiatrist
Gayford (1979). He wrote that men's violent behavior is a reaction to
women's behavior. Supported by his clinical experiences, he concluded his observations in a typology of the abused women as
"inadequate", "provocative", or "highly competent":

Inadequate wives: These are women who grew up under difficult
social circumstances and had endured more than most people. Their
marriages are an extension, and repetition, of the patterns found in
the original families: early marriage due to pregnancy, unstable
finances, and an alcohol-abusing husband. It is often difficult to
determine how much of these women's inadequacy had been
precipitated by the repeated episodes of violence; an inadequate
woman becomes more so under these circumstances, Gayford
remarks. He refers to this "type of family" as "problem families".

Provocative wives: According to Gayford, there are many ways in which women can be provocative and thus cause friction in a marital relationship. Inadequacy has already been mentioned. Overcontrolling behavior and being sexually provocative are other examples. A sexual provocation, especially when coupled with morbid jealousy, can be an extremely dangerous combination, as Gayford further comments.

Highly competent wives: According to Gayford, it is difficult to see how this type of woman becomes a battered wife, as she has often been brought up in a protective environment, has a good education, and holds a responsible job. However, some related problems are eventually observed. The highly competent wife is frequently her husband's intellectual superior, forcing him to rely on her for help in his career. The withdrawal of this help leaves him in a subordinate position, a position which he finds very uncomfortable (Gayford 1979).

In the analysis by Snell and others (1964), and Gayford (1979), women are indirectly made responsible for men's brutality against them. Women as mothers are viewed as the causes behind the disturbed psyche of the violent men, and women as wives are held responsible for situations which arise where a man uses violence against his female partner.

The first Swedish doctoral thesis on woman battering (Bergman 1987) further develops Gayford's observations. At the emergency ward of a large hospital in the vicinity of Stockholm, 98 women who over an eight-month period sought surgical treatment for injuries they incurred after beatings by their husbands or former husbands were asked if they were willing to participate in a treatment program and research project. In addition to the medical treatment, the treatment program included a series of supportive sessions with counselors and psychiatrists. 49 women accepted and thus constituted the study group. After one week, 12 of these women had dropped out, and after one year, 22 women remained (Bergman 1987 p. 12). Of the 49 original women, 51% were high consumers of alcohol, 70% of their men were alcoholics, and both were intoxicated during about 50% of the violent incidents. Eight of the women had or had previously had other drug problems, and 25 used tranquillizers (Bergman 1987 pp. 21-24). Despite the fact that the study's self-selected sample of battered women according to the project leader "to a great degree represented the worst off of battered women" (Brismar, Jansson, and Larsson 1988), the sample was treated as if it were representative, and the findings were generalized to apply to battered women in general. This led to protests from the Scandinavian women's movement.

The women were tested by means of a standardized personality test (Comprehensive Psychopathological Rating Scale), and all of Gayford's (1979) categories of wives were found. It was established that "there is no doubt that a large group of the battered wives in the present study could be labeled as "inadequate wives" according to Gayford's terminology. These women seem to be predestined to become battered wives by their social history and present social situation" (Bergman 1987 p. 27). The group "provocative wives" was found as well. The study states that "the provocative wife is vivacious and energetic, stimulus-seeking and constantly looking for excitement. Her self-confidence is good and she has a type of behavior that the medical and social services and the courts get tired of. When asked, she admits provocation – often simply to create excitement" (Bergman 1987 pp. 27-28). The "highly competent women" were blatantly missing from among the 49 women in the study. "These women are able to deal with their problems themselves" (Bergman 1987 p. 28).

When it comes to understanding human reactions, it is not particularly uncommon to assume that a person's behavior, in this case the man's, is a reaction to another person's behavior, in this case the woman's. On the contrary, we often in our daily lives view our feelings as conditions that result from a provocation or as conditions that befall us. We use expressions such as "you make me mad" or "I think that it is her boss's complaints that have made her so desperate", when we try to understand our own or someone else's emotional responses. When we say "you make me mad", we are at the same time stating that it is the object of our anger and not we ourselves that is responsible for our anger. When this type of everyday rhetoric is used in a scientific thesis, battered women are held responsible for the battering they are subjected to, whereas the men are exempted from responsibility. This way of perceiving the relationship between perpetrator and victim is offensive to the Swedish sense of justice. Bergman's thesis has also been sharply criticized for contributing to the oppression of women (Lundgren 1988 pp. 101-117).

When studying these contributions to the definition of woman battering by researchers from the individual psychological and psychiatric perspectives of human behavior, it is surprising to observe how much energy is invested in trying to understand the men's behavior by means of studying the personality traits of the women. In a survey of 52 studies of woman battering, the American researchers Hotaling and Sugarman (1986) found no support for such suppositions. It was not a woman's personality, or her gender role, or her social status that decreased or increased the risk that just she would be battered. Possible differences in personality and symptomology between battered and non-battered women were *consequences* of the battering rather than *causes* of it. In one aspect, however, there was a distinction between these groups. The battered women had to a greater degree witnessed the battering of their own mothers by their fathers (Hotaling and Sugarman 1986 pp. 101–124).

To sum up, in the tradition of individual psychology and psychiatry, both the battering men and the battered women are pathologized. The marriage is viewed as a harmonious and functional institution, and disharmony in the marriage setting is interpreted as personal failures due to personality imperfection. This perspective has been harshly criticized, not least of all by proponents of the modern women's movement and feminist reseachers.

Sociological research on woman battering

In sociological research on women battering, the emphasis has been on social factors, and there are many studies of the relationship between social background factors and violence. In this research, sociologists Straus and Gelles and their fellow researchers at the Family Research Laboratory at the University of New Hampshire, have played a prominent role. In 1975 and 1985, they conducted National Family Violence Surveys. In the first survey, a representative sample of 2,143 families were interviewed and in the second survey, 6,002.

These two studies resulted in improved research in the field of family violence in three primary ways. First, the 1975 study (Straus, Gelles and Steinmetz 1980) represented an attempt to measure the incidence of violence in a large and representative sample of American families. Second, the availability of data on a representative sample enabled researchers to move beyond the individual psychological perspective of woman battering that was dominant in the 1960s. Third, these surveys broke the tradition of basing research on interviews with battered women, since about half of the respondents were husbands and half were wives. Even if the value of the collected data is somewhat limited due to the fact that these husbands and wives are not members of the same households, the breakthrough of studies on perpetrators as well as victims was of critical importance (Straus,

Gelles, and Steinmetz 1980; Gelles and Straus 1988; Straus and Gelles 1990).

The National Family Violence Surveys used an instrument developed by Straus and Gelles to measure family violence: The Conflict Tactics Scales (CTS). As its name implies, the CTS is designed to measure a variety of behaviors resorted to in conflict situations involving family members. The tactics fall into three general modes: rational discussion, termed Reasoning; verbal or nonverbal acts that symbolically hurt the other, termed Verbal Aggression; and the use of physical aggression, termed Violence. The subjects of the interview were asked:

> No matter how well a couple get along, there are times when they disagree, get annoyed with the other person, or just have spats or fights because they're in a bad mood or tired or for some other reason. They also use many different ways of trying to settle their differences. I'm going to read some things that you and your (spouse/partner) might do when you have an argument. I would like you to tell me how many times (once, twice, 3–5 times, 6–10 times, 11–20 times or more than 20 times) in the past 12 month you:
>
> – discussed an issue calmly
> – got information to back up your/his/her side of things
> – brought in, or tried to bring in, someone to help settle things
> – insulted or swore at him/her/you
> – sulked or refused to talk about an issue
> – stomped out of the room or house or yard
> – cried
> – did or said something to spite him/her/you
> – threatened to hit or hit or kicked something
> – threw or smashed or hit or kicked something
> – threw something at him/her/ you
> – pushed, grabbed or shoved him/her/you
> – slapped him/her/you
> – kicked, bit or hit him/her/you with a fist
> – hit or tried to hit him/her/you with something
> – beat him/her/you up
> – choked him/her/you
> – threatened him/her/you with a knife or gun
> – used a knife or fired a gun.
> (Straus, Gelles and Steinmetz 1980)

The CTS classifies violent acts by *degree of seriousness.* By comparing the two national surveys, Straus and Gelles found that the overall rate of violence by husbands per 1,000 couples declined from 121 to 113 between 1975 and 1985 (Straus and Gelles 1990). Thus, the husband-to-wife violence rate declined by 6.6%, but the decline was not statistically significant. The most important figure, however, was the incidence of severe violence used by husbands, the measure used as an indicator of wife beating. It showed that more than three out of every hundred women were severely assaulted by their partners in 1985. If this rate is correct, it means that about 1.8 million American women were beaten by their partners that year (Straus and Gelles 1990). Since no corresponding figures are available for Swedish women, it is impossible to make any comparisons from a Swedish point of view.

The work of Straus and Gelles and their fellow researchers provide a large body of evidence suggesting that the major causes of physical violence in the family are to be found in certain basic features of the American family, and in the American society as a whole. Among these features are male dominance in the family and the society, the presence of legal violent acts such as capital punishment, and illegal violence seen in the high rate of violence in the streets and millions of people living in poverty in one of the wealthiest societies in human history (Straus and Gelles 1990). In many respects, the perspective of sociologists in the field of woman battering is close to that of the feminists. Nevertheless, the research of Straus and Gelles has been subjected to serious criticism from feminist scholars.

This critique is based on the authors' use of family as a unit for analysis which, according to the critics, drew attention away from the gender-specific nature of wife beating. The critics also challenged the use of quantitative methods instead of qualitative in-depth interviewing (Dobash and Dobash 1979; Breines and Gordon 1983; Russell 1988).

Some of the results aroused particular indignation. Analysis of the 1975 as well as the 1985 survey revealed that the rates of violence by wives were remarkably similar to the rates of violence by husbands, findings that were inconsistent with the extremely low rate of assault by women outside the family (Straus and Gelles 1990). Feminists labeled this analysis as poor, due to methodological errors and due to the failure to determine whether the women had used the violence in self-defence (Breines and Gordon 1983). Researchers of the National Family Violence Survey were viewed as anti-feminists and were sometimes shouted down when they tried to present their work in public settings. One of the female researchers was the victim of a bomb threat and received threats over the phone. In the latest report, Straus comments on these events:

The intensity of the feminist attack was an outgrowth of a double transgression – the sin of reporting evidence that women assault their spouses and children and the sin of using quantitative methods. The first of these sins, in the view of the critics, is an outgrowth of the second. (Straus and Gelles 1990 pp. 11–12)

According to Blumer, the process through which a phenomenon emerges as a social problem can be traced to the claims made and the responding activities to these claims (Blumer 1971). As noted, such activities are not idyllic undertakings, but rather entail conflicts and fights.

Unlike the researchers who studied woman battering in an individual psychological perspective, sociologists perceived marriage as an institution which contains the possibilities of conflict. "No matter how well a couple gets along, there are times when they disagree", as stated in the introduction of the National Violence Survey. Accordingly, a person who fights with his or her spouse should not be pathologized. Some expressions of disagreement, though, are considered illegitimate, among them the use of physical violence.

The social psychological meaning of woman battering – a summary

The battering of women within a marriage is an age-old phenomenon. Accordingly, the female experience of male violent behavior constitutes a substantial part of women's history. Our modern conception of woman battering is thus the result of a process of definition and delimitation of the phenomenon, in part over the past twenty years. The problem has been dealt with within the framework of three different perspectives, namely, the perspectives of the women's movement and feminism, of individual psychology and of sociology.

All of these perspectives take a negative view of violence, and see it as something definitely not appropriate within a marriage. The various perspectives emphasize different aspects of the phenomenon and identify the central issues differently. For example, those working within the individual psychology perspective locate the causes of the violent events discussed here in the personality characteristics of the *victim* (Snell et al. 1964; Gayford 1979; Bergman 1987) or of the *offender* (Schultz 1960; Faulk 1974; Cullberg 1984; Gondolf 1985; Hamberger and Hastings 1986). According to the feminist perspective, the root of male violent behavior is not to be found in the personality traits of the victim, nor in those of the offender. In a feminist view, woman battering is an unambiguous and brutal example of male dominance and female subordination (Dobash and Dobash 1979; Yllö 1990; Stanko 1985). Central to the feminist analysis is a focus on the *consequences* that woman battering has on its victims (Walker 1978; 1979; Pagelow 1981; Araldsen and Clasen 1983; Christensen 1984). In order to determine the *causes of the violence,* sociological research concentrates on the scope of the violence and on the relationship of the violence to variables such as alcohol, social status, and stress (Gelles 1974; Gelles 1979; Gelles and Straus 1988; Straus et al 1980; Straus and Gelles 1990; Finkelhor 1983). The modern women's movement has played a prominent role in the changing of battered women's understanding of themselves and has played a significant role for the general cultural understanding of the phenomenon as an expression of the male oppression of women.

"Woman battering", I will conclude, is not just an action or an event. I have put the term in quotes to emphasize that it is not an objective event that carries with it predetermined meanings. Rather, it is an interpretation rendered within various frameworks, frameworks that shape and mold the reactions that both the woman and man experiencing battering as battered and batterer and others will have. These shared reactions are made possible by the shared language system in which we all operate.

The study of "woman battering" has to a great extent been synonymous with the study of "wife battering", with no distinction being made between them. This has resulted in the focus being put on the gender-specific character of "woman battering", in a most elucidating way. Unintentionally, this focus has resulted in neglect of the fact that in the case of wife battering, the female victim and the male perpetrator are in a special relationship to each other, namely, a marriage. Indirectly it means, however, that it is possible to conclude from the various accounts of "woman battering" that there are also divergent views of marriage and of the link between marriage and the violent event.

The underlying conception of marriage from an individual psychological view is a harmonious one, where expressions like "a haven in a heartless world" or "they lived happily ever after" apply. In such a context, the violent events reflect one or two cases of individual pathology. The sociological approach to the phenomenon of marital violence, on the other hand, presupposes conflicts within a family. Married spouses, parents, and siblings may all be involved in conflicts. Disagreements, antagonisms, and attempts to influence each other are seen as natural aspects of family life. In extreme situations, unjustifiable means such as violence are used in the struggle to influence a situation in the desired direction. Finally, the feminist perspective describes marriage as a hierarchy, characterized by male dominance and female subordination. Violence by men against women constitutes a "natural" consequence of this hierarchical order.

Defining woman battering

In spite of all the efforts made to develop a clear definition of the concept of woman abuse and battering, a satisfactory result has not been attained. In other words, a clear and useful definition, one that is universally adopted, has not emerged. The disappointment over the apparently insurmountable problems in this type of search for an abstract, general, and normative definition that has dominated the field, is expressed by Gelles and Straus (1988) as follows:

> Twenty years of discussion, debate, and action have led us to conclude that there will never be an accepted or acceptable definition of abuse, because abuse is not a scientific or clinical term. Rather, it is a political concept. Abuse is essentially any act that is considered deviant or harmful by a group large enough or with sufficient political power to enforce the definition. (Gelles and Straus 1988 p.54)

One possible means of avoiding the difficulties with a *normative* definition of woman battering is to include both the *definition* of woman battering and the *process of definition* in research on woman battering. In this way, we get around the compulsion to superimpose an "external" definition on a social incident which has already been defined by the parties involved and by outside observers such as the police, social workers, lawyers, researchers, or neighbors. Obviously, we all share certain knowledge about male violent behavior against women, knowledge that provides us with sufficient social competence to identify an act of violence as battering, or maybe as a fight, or as some other form of violence.

Considering this choice of research subject, the researcher's task becomes one of delimiting, clarifying, and presenting that which is defined and perceived as woman battering in our society and our culture. In other words, the researcher must study the socio-psychological aspects of these actions. He or she must try to identify the distinctive features of the actions, try to identify the rules and conventions used by the social actors to generate their behavior, and try to understand how the involved parties themselves make sense of what has happened. This is the topic of my study.

The issues

It has been suggested (Harré and Secord 1972) that all actions, whether verbal or otherwise, should be explained with reference to the actor's *social competence*. The possession of social competence limits the acts one is able to perform in social situations and determines what is acceptable as the correct performance of these acts. The methodological challenge in a study based on this view of the origin of human behavior would not be to search for laws of causality to explain human behavior, but rather to try to identify the *rules* and *conventions* adopted by social actors to generate their behavior (Harré 1979; Harré 1983; Potter and Wetherell 1987). According to this suggestion, human actions within a culture are considered to be far more than mere bodily movements which can be easily described and catalogued. The social world can only be understood if we explore human behavior in the setting in which it occurs. Movements and behavior have meaning only in the context of specific, and often very local, social conventions.

My study relies heavily on the assumption that individuals possess social knowledge, which enables them both to act and relate accounts of their actions as explanations or justifications of what has occurred. It is also based on the assumption that individuals act and interpret social action on the basis of how they define a situation. The principal method used in my study consists of attempting to gain access to and to analyze the narrative accounts of what actually happened by the men and women involved in acts of repeated marital violence as batterer and battered.

In my view, a husband's violent behavior towards his wife is not to be regarded as an individually determined action, caused by an irresistible impulse of aggressiveness or by a pathological personality, but rather as a cultural artifact. The significance of the act for the couple involved, however, will be individually as well as relationally grounded, which means that the act of marital violence takes place in, and creates a meaning within, the individual as well as in the marital life of the parties involved. Consequently, how the husband and wife interpret the violent action would be a product of their individually, relationally, and culturally determined modes and expectations of what their own marital life would bring. The concept of "marriage" is here, and below, used to include legal marriages as well as what has been known as common-law marriages or cohabitation with the intention of living in an intimate couple relationship but without a formal marriage licence.

The marital act of violence

In my understanding, the link between violent behavior and the setting in which it occurs, that is, the marriage, is of fundamental significance for the understanding of the violent act. A violent act committed within a marriage is in turn a *marital act*. If this distinction is not made, the link between the man's violent outburst and the marriage would be broken. This would severely reduce the possibility for the actors as well as observers to understand what has happened. The link between action and context is of fundamental significance for the understanding of the violent act, as well as for the understanding of all human action. Take something out of context – and it becomes meaningless. Put it in a new context – and it means something else.

According to prevailing conceptions of developments in men's and women's lives, assumed to have occurred over the past 50 years, Sweden has been transformed from a society in which sex-segregation was a manifestation of the social order into a society where the integration of the sexes within many spheres is an explicit societal goal. The Swedish society is also seen to have developed from a society in which men's dominance and women's subordination were legitimated by a notion of the superiority of men's capacity and skills, to one where obvious male dominance is seen as insidious (Haavind 1984; 1985). These widely expressed perceptions in Swedish society are significant for the development of rules that constitute different types of relationships between men and women. This is especially true for the institution of marriage.

Not to preempt my own study, but rather to identify the object of it, I contend here that the rule that constitutes a marriage in the context of Swedish society and influences how men and women will deal with violent incidents, in all probability could be summarized by the following statement: Violence is *a morally questionable marital act.*

The principal characteristic of this study is my twofold effort to:
– identify and describe the distinctive feature of the morally questionable marital act of woman battering, as it appeared and was performed by the men in the marital life of the spouses I interviewed;
– and to understand how the involved individuals made sense of this act, that is, how they defined and interpreted, and explained and justified it.

My overall ambition with the study is to contribute to the identification of the rules and conventions generating the parties' behavior during the process of the violent act, as they are revealed in the parties' descriptions, explanations, and justifications of the marital violent act.

This study has almost exclusively relied on the social knowledge of men and women who are involved in repeated acts of marital woman battering. The information I have sought has focused on three different issues:

– my informants' understanding of what happened in connection with and during the violent events;

– my informants' understanding of themselves, their partners, and their relationships;

– my informants' life-histories, and their understanding of how these histories may help them explain and understand what happened to them in their lives and marriages.

A note on the organization of the text

Before I continue, I will briefly describe what will be found in the following chapters.

In the next chapter, I will deepen the discussion of "the marriage" as the social context that conceptually determines the marital violent act and that at the same time forms the setting in which it occurs. My aim here is to evolve a theoretical perspective for further analysis of the narrative accounts of marital violent acts.

The chapter that follows is devoted to the "act of research", that is, the methodological considerations of my study. These considerations concern two principal issues: Gaining access to the narrative accounts of the questionable marital act of violence from the batterer as well as from the battered woman, two individuals who live together in a marriage, and the analysis of these accounts.

The narrative accounts of the violent act that piece by piece were given to me during numerous interviews, revealed a structure that can be named as *traditional* (Ong 1982). It contained a beginning, a middle, and an end, and a logic holding the story together. The narratives were shaped as "dramas" with three parts, beginning with a *pre-history,* progressing through the *violent incident,* and ending with the *aftermath.* Each of these parts are described and analyzed in separate chapters. Thus, the description of the violent incident is introduced with a short chapter where these incidents are described in figures.

In the final chapter, "The Violent Marriage", I briefly summarize my study, and bring the text to a close by discussing the possibilities for transforming the violent marriage into a non-violent marriage.

2

Marriage – The Scene of Marital Violence

Introduction

A man is yelling at a woman in a public place. His behavior is perceived as quite unpleasant and threatening. The entire situation is very disturbing. People's sympathies lie with the woman. Should we intervene? Then someone informs them, "That's Mr. and Mrs. Anderson". As if one, the passersby all let out a sigh of relief. They do not have to intervene after all. Neither of the parties receives much sympathy now. On the contrary. The onlookers dissociate themselves from both the man and the woman and someone decries them, "Strange people, why do they fight in public, why don't they save it for home?"

A commonplace incident such as this provides us with an example of how a misinterpretation of the relationship between a man and a woman can lead to dramatic differences in people's perception of a situation. A man who behaves in a threatening manner against an unknown woman breaks the prevailing rules for aggressive outbursts in our culture. If it turns out that he is the woman's husband, however, the same rule violation has not occurred.

If Mr. Anderson had not been Mr. Anderson, but rather Police Commissioner Anderson in the performance of his job, the event would have had a different import. A Police Commissioner has the right to use violence in his job, although not unchecked. The performance of his job is regulated by rules which determine the boundaries for his behavior in physical struggle situations. If these boundaries are transgressed, the violence then loses its legitimacy.

The description of the incident involving Mr. and Mrs. Anderson illustrates the crucial role that a social category, namely, marriage, plays in the understanding of woman battering. Marriage is the social category which *conceptually determines the violence* that Mrs. Anderson is subjected to. When Mr. Anderson acts threateningly against his wife, this act belongs to the category of marital acts. When he behaves threateningly towards an unknown woman, this act would belong to an entirely different category, namely, the category of actions between strangers.

For Mrs. Anderson to understand what type of event she experienced, it is not sufficient to make a simple categorization of what happened. The incident would have had different meanings for her, as well as for any witnesses, depending on whether she had been assaulted by an unknown man in a park or had been assaulted by her husband in their shared home. She cannot understand what happened to her other than in light of the *social context* in which the event unfolded. The essence of this second conclusion, drawn from the description of the incident between Mr. and Mrs. Anderson, is that what happens in the social world can be understood only by exploring the human behavior in the setting in which it occurs. In this case, it is marriage that constitutes the setting: a violent act committed within a marriage is a marital act.

The third and final conclusion possible to draw from the above incident is that the use of violence as social action is surrounded by rules that determine the boundaries of its legitimacy. In his comprehensive work, *The Civilizing Process,* the German sociologist and civilization critic Norbert Elias (1978) presents a study on how the rules we apply to restrict the use of violence between human beings have undergone a great change seen in a historical perspective. Elias shows that a change has been occurring over many generations in people's affective and control structures towards a more rigid and differentiated control. For example, 15th century people were violent in war as well as in love. Feelings were expressed directly in a way that we today generally only observe in children. Feelings were ventilated in more uninhibited fashion, more directly and openly than has since been the case. Today, we are more restrained and considerate. Current legislation strictly regulates physical struggle between people (Elias 1978). The limits of legitimacy determine the nature of the violence which is permissible in certain contexts and establish the rules for how it is to be exercised. That which is possible for a person in a certain context is impossible in another context. That which is possible for one person is impossible for another.

In this introduction, I have attempted to argue that in a study on violence against women in a marriage, there are several reasons for directing particular attention to the link between the action in question and the social context in which it occurs, namely, the marriage. I do not wish to enter into an extended theoretical discussion here on the nature of marital life. Instead, I will briefly present some of the theoretical background of this work in relation to issues essential to the understanding of marital interaction. This discussion is both a precondition for an adequate appreciation of the subsequent analysis of marital woman battering and a part of the outcome of this analysis. I will introduce four aspects of marital life that I found central to the understanding of the process of making sense of what happens, and central to reaching conclusions about the effect of the event undergone by all the individuals involved.

First and foremost, a marriage is an example of a phenomenon organizing social relations between the sexes. As they enter the world of marital life, the lives of the man and the woman are radically transformed. It seems reasonable here to describe the change in terms of a more or less radical reorganization of the parties' everyday life. In this sense, it is possible to view marriage as a *social organization*. This social organization could be described as a composition of social relations between man and woman who are classified as "husband" and "wife".

In the previous chapter, I discussed the idea that all people possess a store of *social knowledge* (Harré and Secord 1972) that enables them to act and determines what will be an acceptable and correct performance of the act in question. A socially competent person knows how to behave in particular socially determined situations. Most people know what is expected of them as customers at the post office, at the grocer's, or on a train journey. If we observe people in these situations, we discover that the overwhelming majority act apparently without difficulty in accordance with the underlying social rules that constitute the situation in question. We often take compliance with these rules for granted, and only become aware of them when they are violated. A person who enters a post office and inquires after the diningcar would most certainly be perceived as deviant. The average person, however, is aware of a set of social rules which enables him or her to act proficiently and rationally, and to display that proficiency and rationality.

A marriage is an example of a phenomenon which is determined by social rules. A man and a woman who live in a marital relationship must take into consideration those rules which reflect norms and conceptions of how a marriage should be. The concept of rules should not be seen here primarily as a commentary *about* actions; instead, it is the rules that *constitute* the action in question. In this sense, a marriage is its marital rules.

In the previous chapter, I assumed that the rule constituting a marriage in the context of the Swedish society and influencing how men and women will deal with violent incidents within that marriage could be summarized in the statement, *Violence is a morally questionable* marital act. This rule allows broad parameters within which incidents of violence within the marriage can be interpreted. It provides considerable space for the individual couple to develop their own understanding of what happened, and to reach their own conclusions about the effect of this event on their marriage.

The remaining three of these aspects concern the *social psychological meaning* of marriage, the *interactional issues* of marital life, and, finally the *issues of organizing* the joint life.

The social psychological meaning of marriage: To provide identity and life-style

In the feminist literature (Pateman 1988; Bernard 1982; Barker 1978), marriage has been discussed in terms of a *status contract,* that is, an agreement between two parties to accept a status determined by external forces. It is not my intention to delve deeper into the analysis of marriage in terms of contract theory or to discuss the feasibility of this approach. In my opinion, though, the concept of status contract captures a central marital dimension. This concept suggests an important characteristic of marital life, namely, its profound link with the parties' individual life histories. When a man and a woman enter into a marriage they attain marital status. This means that they are *transformed into something* by the marriage – husband and wife – and in the long run often father and mother. The individual psychological import of this is found in the fact that the parties define themselves as spouses, that is, they define themselves in relation to another person. A person cannot be a spouse without there being another spouse. In addition, marriage provides a way of life for a woman and a man that is sanctioned by society.

To become someone who lives in a couple relationship as spouse is something that is a natural part of many people's lives. Even if a large number of people end their marriages, a great proportion of these eventually enter into new marriages. Few people seem prepared to discard the marital life-style, despite the fact that they do not seldom discard their own marital partner. The binding force of marriage seems to be more compelling than the individual partner.

One can gain a notion of the weight and type of significance that the marital way of life has in our culture by studying the history of divorce. In his comprehensive work, *Road to Divorce,* the historian Stone (1990) describes the history of divorce in England between 1530 and 1987. His work reveals that during the first part of the period 1887–1987, the most ardent proponents of marriage were the church and the English league of housewives. Both bodies campaigned – from somewhat different perspectives – against a liberal divorce law. The church argued that marriage constituted a guarantee for the upholding of morals, order, and security for the coming generations, and the housewives argued that marriage was a necessary protection for women. A liberal divorce law could lead to the degradation of women by enabling husbands to leave their wives whenever they became infatuated with someone else (Stone 1990 pp. 383-396). During the latter part of this period, women *advocated* a liberalization of the legislation. The notion that the essence of marriage was love and affinity between the spouses had become more widely disseminated. Prior to the 1930s, a marriage could only be dissolved on grounds of infidelity; after the 1937 reform in the divorce laws, desertion and cruelty were added as grounds for divorce (Stone 1990 pp. 397–422).

Becoming a married couple is a far-reaching and profound experience and is a continuously on-going action – a marriage is never "completed". "Marriage in our society is a dramatic act in which two strangers come together and redefine themselves", as sociologists Berger and Kellner have written (Berger and Kellner 1970 p.53).

During the uniting phase, the two parties are required to abandon some of their individuality for the sake of joint action. The individuals may later be compelled to give up a part of this union – this time, for the sake of individuality. In my opinion, a vigorous marriage is characterized by constant movement between individuality and union, where the contracting parties may be separate and different but retain the communality that the joint marital project affords them.

The dramatic act of marriage can be described in terms of the formation by the partners of a *joint marital project*. They each contribute to this unique formation of marital life-style from the starting point of their individual biologically, and socially determined conditions. The relationship between the spouses is thus characterized by the fact that from their distinct positions, the two people become each other's collaborators in the formation of the joint project. The success of the joint project depends on how well this collaboration functions.

To describe a marriage in terms of a project necessitates the introduction of the dimension of time. Marriage is not only viewed in terms of the given or current situation, but more accurately *in light of its future.* The project is the expression of the marriage's goals and contents in constant fluctuation, where there is a constant interplay between the marital scene and the acts performed on it. To participate in this cooperative project given the actors' preconditions means that they are neither helpless victims of a predestined fate, nor can either alone form the ultimate perfect future.

As the spouses interact, they design a unique structure for the marital project. They create a fundamental form of social organization. In other words, they create a social order formulated, refuted, and reconstituted through interaction. Violent behavior constitutes just such an interactional component and leads to a certain *social order.*

As previously mentioned, the feminist analysis of woman battering focuses on the hierarchical power structure of the traditional marriage, with the man in the dominant and the woman in the subordinate position. The feminist analysis starts with an analysis on the societal level, and it states that the oppression a battered woman is subjected to by her male partner is a brutal example of male dominance and female subordination.

When I view the presence of male violent behavior as a constituting factor of marital life, I view the correlation between male violence and marital social order somewhat differently than does the feminist approach. My understanding of this correlation is that of a *dialectic process,* not one of a linear cause-effect correlation. To my understanding, a husband's use of violence towards his wife, and the way she reacts to it, produces a social order as well as reflects an already existing social order in the surrounding society.

My ideas about the joint marital project have been influenced by Jean-Paul Sartre's observations on human existence. Sartre (1968) said that the nature of human life is both regressive and progressive, and that the manner in which we form our lives is an expression of the fact that our lives are determined by certain preconditions which are, however, possible to transcend. That which makes a person unique in relation to others is his or her basic choice of approach to existence. Sartre refers to these fundamental choices as the principal human project (Sartre 1968).

Sartre's analysis makes it possible to identify not only the joint marital project but also the *individual life projects* as the essential features of a marriage. The marriage does not only consist of the marital project, but of the two individual life projects as well. These two types of projects are in constant interaction with each other. For many people, marriage is a necessary component of life. Such an attitude would ensure the marital project a strong position in these people's lives. For others, the marital project is of less importance for their individual projects. The relationship between the joint project and the individual projects can thus take different forms, thereby creating completely different bases for spousal assessments and integration of what happens in the marriage.

The mutual dependence of the individual projects and the marital project lends a special nature to all occurrences within the marriage, not least of all in conflictory situations. This mutual dependence may place the partners in paradoxical situations. Let us imagine a situation where one of the spouse's will prevails at a given time, and where this spouse perceives himself or herself as the victor and the other spouse as the loser. Thus, one spouse's victory, at the other's expense, may in all probability lead to a loss, even for the joint marital project – and then indirectly to a loss for the victorious party, due to the mutual dependence of the two kinds of projects.

In the case of divorce, this mutual dependence of the two kinds of projects has an impact. Besides the dissolution of the marriage, the two individual life projects are affected. After the termination of a difficult marriage that weighed heavily on his or her life project, an individual may experience great relief and may "bloom" in many respects. However, a termination always contains some element of loss. All the hopes and expectations connected with a marriage are lost; the way of life and identity are lost; that which the marriage "turned one into" is lost (for a further discussion, see Kohler Riessman 1990). If that which is lost upon separation has been significant for the individual's life, a separation or threat of separation may be experienced by that individual as a total catastrophe, even if the joint marital project had been problematic.

The dynamics of marital interaction

There are certain aspects of marital life which are fundamental to every marriage. These aspects can be described in terms of *fundamental interactional themes* concerning fundamental processes in the couple's joint life. Every couple must undergo these processes and their outcome constitutes a distinctive feature of a marriage.

As is true of all human relations, *trust* is basic to the marital project. What characterizes a trusting relationship is difficult to express in words. I would prefer to maintain that one *lives* a trusting relationship. Any attempt to describe this verbally easily becomes banal in expressions such as "she means more to me than anything else in the world" or "he is such a fantastic person". In interactional terminology, trust can be defined as a feeling that the other is on your side, that the other person is looking out for your best and will not deliberately hurt you.

Defective trust is easier to express. It often takes the form of the parties saying they are unsure about each other, where one party perceives the other as deceitful and unreliable. The trust theme is especially manifested in the realm of sexual relations and jealousy.

During the formation phase of the marriage, the question of trust is also central. Once the marital project has been established and the relationship between the parties confirmed in a positive way, trust exists more as a resonance in the relationship, without it requiring much of either party's energies. The individuals simply expect not to be let down or abandoned.

Another central theme in marriage is nurturing, that of *who takes care of whom,* and who helps whom with what. This theme could be depicted in the following imaginary dialogue between two women: "He is fantastic at knowing when I am tired and then he takes care of me. For my part, I try to fuss over him a little extra when he comes home after a long day at the job", a woman could say who lives in a marriage characterized by mutual nurturing. "He doesn't notice much. I want him to take care of me and to see when I am sad and when I need him", a woman might say who lives in a marriage more characterized by the lack of mutual nurturing.

Finally, the third central interactional theme involves power, who *decides* what, and who shall *control* whom and what. Three strategies are described in the literature for the development of interactional patterns for regulating power and control in the family, namely, *direct confrontation, establishing rules,* or *determination of joint principles* for what is valued and given priority in the marital project (Cromwell and Olsson 1975).

To use violence against another human being is to exert power over that person. Power is defined in many different ways in the social sciences (Lukes 1974). Therefore, it is warranted to define the concept of power more closely before using it in the following presentation.

In my view, the concept of power ought to be perceived as a *relational concept* for describing the relationship between two persons. This notion is not the same as the one reflecting a linear thinking, where it is maintained that power is a type of resource or a proficiency that a person possesses or is bestowed with, and then uses against a weaker person. This definition of power implies that power is not perceived as a formal property of a relationship possible to be determined *externally* by means of an operational definition, but rather is linked to its substance and to the context in which it is exerted (See further Foucault 1981).

This view corresponds to the one mentioned above of a husband's use of violence towards his wife and the way she reacts to it as a dialectic process which produces and reflects marital social order.

When one studies separate incidents which are limited in time, it may be difficult to analyze the interactional pattern in the relationship in terms of the power aspect. In my opinion, this applies even when studying an event such as a husband's use of violence against his wife. It is first when the sequence of events that constitute the entire course of the violent act is studied – its pre-history, the violent outburst itself, and its aftermath – that it becomes possible to identify the type of power being exerted, and how this use of power defines the marriage in question. To use violence against a person with whom one shares a close relationship, however, is not only a question of power. It is also a question of abusing this person's trust and expresses a total lack of nurturing.

The most common ways of organizing everyday marital life

In research on families and couples, two main types of social organization of marriages can be discerned. This classification is based on Gregory Bateson's observation that human interaction follows two main lines, one where people relate to each other *symmetrically* and one where they define their roles in a complementary manner (Bateson 1958). The symmetrical form of interaction is based on similarity, and the parties tend to mirror each other's behavior so that their communication becomes similar, whereas complementary interaction is based on dissimilarity. These two patterns of interaction are frequently used in the categorization of families (See further: Watzlawick 1967; Jackson 1968; Hoffman 1981).

In its most pronounced form, the complementary pattern of living together is represented by *the traditional marriage*. This lifestyle is characterized by a clear-cut division of labor between the sexes, where the woman cares for the home, and the man operates in the world beyond (Haavind 1985).

In a symmetrically organized pattern of living together, the category of gender is not quite as decisive for the exact division of labor and of responsibility. Instead, the parties negotiate about the organization of the everyday life. The symmetrical marriage has been described in terms of a "marriage of equals" or a "marriage of peers" (Young and Wilmott 1973). It has been viewed as an ideal, as "the future marriage" (Bernard 1982).

The Norwegian social-psychologist, Haavind, contends in an article on changes in the relationship between women and men, that marital life in today's Scandinavia can be described in terms of *social mobility* (Haavind 1984; 1985). The well-defined complementary gender roles are in the process of dissolution, and therefore, couples find themselves in constant negotiations about what gender implies. She believes that we are moving towards greater equalization regarding those properties we associate with masculinity and femininity, but that the sexes basically still relate to one another in the same way as previously. Haavind describes this relationship as follows:

> A modern woman is able to do everything, just as long as she does it subordinately in relation to those men she associates with. Her chances for being reaffirmed positively as a woman, that is, to be highly valued, are greatest if she herself presents this relative subordination as something other than subordination. (Haavind 1985 p. 21)

To an outside observer, such a marriage might appear to be organized along symmetrical principles. Haavind argues that the resulting form of marital project can be designated as *quasi-egalitarian,* and constitutes a form of complementary pattern in that it is based on the principles of female subordination and male dominance.

This leaves us with three patterns of social organization of marriage, namely, the traditional, the symmetrical, and the quasi-egalitarian. According to Haavind (1985), the quasi-egalitarian organized marriage is a common marital form in Scandinavia, at least among middle-class couples.

Agreement and disagreement about the organization of everyday life

One aspect seldom mentioned in the categorization of marriages based on the organization of everyday marital life, is whether or not there is agreement on the way of organization. It is my view that such information is crucial, not least of all in a study of marital violence. For example, two marriages, both traditionally organized, could provide two completely different scenes for marital action depending on whether both parties in the marriage agree with the arrangement or not.

According to what I have learned from this study, there are two types of conflicts related to this issue. The conflict latent in the marriage where there is agreement about how the marital project will be organized is described here in terms of a conflict about which actions are compatible with and which are incompatible with what the couple has defined, delimited, and agreed upon with regard to their marriage. In the *accordant marriage,* conflicts may arise as to where the boundaries are drawn. Men and women in accordant marriages are in basic agreement about curtailing their own personal freedom in order to attain something together. But what this means in practice can be interpreted differently by the two parties.

In those marriages where *disagreement* prevails as to the fundamental organization of the marital project, the situation is the reverse. The latent conflict here could be described in terms of the continuous possibility of an antagonism between the individual and the marital projects. Such couples are discordant with regard to the curtailment of personal freedom, since they have not succeeded in agreeing about the common project in such a way that both parties are able to view it as an asset for their individual life projects.

In addition to the antagonism between the life and marital projects, there is also a constant insecurity in the discordant marriage about the continued existence of the marital project. When there is discord about the most fundamental aspects of marital life, fantasies of flight and separation become part of the marital project. Thus, the theme of trust and the theme of caring are continuously and painfully vulnerable in this kind of marriage.

The marriage – scene of marital violence – a summary

In this chapter, I have argued that in a study on violence against women in a marriage, there are several reasons for directing particular attention to the link between the action in question and the social context in which it occurs, namely, the marriage. I have described the modes by which the couples design their marital life in terms of the husband and wife in a joint marital project. Thus, the marriage not only consists of the marital project, but also of two individual life projects.

I found four aspects of marital life to be central to the understanding of the process of how spouses make sense of what happens in their marriage. The first of these aspects concerns the view of marriage as a composition of social relations between the man and the woman; the second, the social, psychological meaning of marriage; the third, the interactional issues of marital life; and the fourth, the issue of how to organize the joint life.

3

The Act of Research

Introduction

The act of research has been described as "those endeavors of a researcher to take her or him from theory to methods, to the empirical world and back again" (Denzin 1978 p.ix). According to this definition, the research act commences with some theoretical study, which yields modes of conceptualization for analyzing and describing the issue to be researched. This theoretical work lays the foundation for the continuous act of research and provides a means or a strategy for the handling of data (Denzin 1978).

In light of the theoretical background of my study and the issues in focus, four methodological tasks are essential, namely:

- to search for informants, with experiences that cover the breadth of marital woman battering,
- to gain access to data about the questionable marital act of violence, from the battering men as well as from the battered women, who live together in a marriage,
- to examine the narrative accounts of marital violence, obtained from interviews with both the batterer and the battered,
- to present an analysis of these accounts in a social science text.

In the following, I will discuss each of these tasks briefly.

The search for informants

Two of the societal institutions that receive direct information about family violence are the police and the social authorities. As the first step in my search for informants, I contacted one of Greater Stockholm's police districts as well as the social welfare offices within this district and requested continuous access to their material over the course of a year.

The police district I chose comprised about 130,000 inhabitants and was known for its high rate of violent criminality. Socio-demographically, the composition of the area was heterogeneous. It contained many older single-family housing areas, relatively large areas with row houses, and several large areas with multi-family apartment buildings built in the 1960s and 1970s. The area was known for its ethnically mixed population from many countries around the world.

Police reports and social files
Over the course of one year, 417 cases of assault and aggravated assault were reported, in which a woman was the victim and a man the perpetrator. In 299 of these cases, the victims and perpetrators were known to each other, and 124 of these involved the type of cases I wanted to study, namely, repeated violence where victim and perpetrator lived or had lived together. Eighty-one of these couples were also known to the social authorities. Moreover, the social workers were aware of a further 29 couples, not known to the police. These 29 couples added to the 124 totaled 153 couples. The first review of the material revealed that twelve of the police cases had to be excluded from the study due to insufficient information in the files. Remaining were 141 cases (Table 3:1). These 141 cases in part underlie the quantitative description of the violent event found in chapter 5, and in part constituted the base from which I chose 20 couples to serve as my informants.

	N	%
Known to the social authorities alone	29	21
Known to the police alone	31	22
Known to both the social authorities and the police	81	57
Total	141	100

Table 3:1. The final sample.

What kind of violent events is it possible to study on the basis of crime reports made to the police?

The police base their assessment of reported violent events on the classification found in the third chapter of the Swedish Criminal Code. In categorizing these violent events, the police look at whether the event can be considered *illegitimate* or not. The police investigation is expected to result in a determination of whether a criminal act has occurred or not, what the charge should be, and against whom there are reasonable grounds for suspecting criminal actions. This means that violent events seen as legitimate never become the object of investigation. In this category, we find verbally aggressive outbursts – if they are not perceived as serious threats – as well as the most minor forms of violence.

In the legal texts, the crimes are classified according to the degree of seriousness into five principal categories:

Molestation: Implies subjecting someone to deliberate minor bodily discomfort, such as slight shoves, to disturbing noise or light, or to the tearing of clothes.

Assault: Implies deliberate infliction of *bodily injury,* disease, or *pain*, placing someone in a powerless or similar condition. Included in bodily injury are sores, swellings, and fractures, and also functional impairments such as paralysis and injuries to sight or hearing. *Disease* may include both physical and mental conditions. Finally, by pain is meant physical suffering that is not minor.

Aggravated assault: An assault that is either *life-threatening* or results in *serious bodily injuries,* or *serious disease* where the perpetrator has used *weapons* or *instruments,* or has shown particular *ruthlessness* or *brutality.*

Regular cases of intentional killing are charged as murder. *Manslaughter* is when someone is killed intentionally but where mitigating circumstances indicate that the act is to be seen as less serious. Both these crimes are thus excluded from my study.

What is of interest here is that in their assessments of the violent actions reported to them, the police make no attempt to classify or evaluate the actions by defining them operationally. On the contrary, the police method of classifying violent events more closely resembles judicial reasoning. This method of classification implies a dissolution of the concept of violence in favor of a system where the event's *social context* is used as the point of departure for the categorization rather than the specific violent behavior itself. What remains is a sort of comprehensive generic concept of violence.

In this perspective, the question "Does a slap constitute battering?" is a completely meaningless question. The answer may be "yes" if the slap resulted in the woman's ear drum exploding. A slap could even be captioned as something more serious than assault if the victim falls to the floor as a result of the slap and is injured so seriously that she later dies. On the other hand, the answer could be "no", if the slap causes only negligible pain and leaves no traces. The police system of categorization into molestation, assault, and aggravated assault draws on judicial terminology and classification practice but at the same time reflects *qualitatively different sociopsychological realities.* Each of the acts are surrounded by different rules and have different consequences for the victims and perpetrators. The central element in the social situation the police label as "assault" is that it concerns an action where the perpetrator through the use of physical violence intentionally inflicts on the victim bodily injury, disease, or pain.

The violence that has been reported to the police and captioned as assault or aggravated assault is that kind of violence which causes serious to medium/minor injuries. The same is true of the 29 cases which were known to the social authorities alone. (Table 3:2)

	No. of cases	Prop. (%)
Facial injuries		
None	23	16
Medium/minor	36	25
Black and blue	48	34
Fractures and other serious injuries	19	14
Information lacking	15	11
Total	**141**	**100**
Bodily injuries		
None	40	28
Medium/minor	41	29
Black and blue	31	22
Fractures and other serious injuries	14	10
Information lacking	15	11
Total	**141**	**100**

Table 3:2 Battered women's injuries.

In summary, it can be stated that the police reports and the files at the welfare offices can be used to study serious violent crimes against women. In those cases where the file material contains insufficient information, it is complemented by means of direct interview with the social workers involved. Nevertheless, information is still lacking, primarily for those 29 cases which were known only to the social authorities.

However, this type of material is not especially well suited to the study of minor physical violence or violence that does not take the form of direct physical violence, such as harassment and inhibiting someone's freedom of movement.

The process of gradual sampling

As already mentioned, the 141 cases of repeated violence, with a female victim and a male perpetrator, where victim and perpetrator lived or had lived together until recently, constituted the basic material for the description of the violent event in quantitative terms. In addition, they constituted the base from which I chose twenty couples to serve as my informants.

In all essentials, the procedure of sampling informants from the 141 couples could be described as a *gradual sampling,* steered by the issues of inquiry. This mode of sampling is related to a principle for sampling known as *theoretically directed sampling* (Glaser and Strauss 1979), a principle that explicitly acknowledges a general sociological perspective or a general subject or problem area as a base for decision-making concerning data collection.

Consequently, it is my conceptualization of woman battering within the marriage as a morally questionable marital act, and the description of "the marriage" as the social context that conceptually determines this act, that constitute one part of the sampling procedure. The issues of research constitute another:

- the identification and description of the distinctive features of marital woman battering
- the understanding of how the involved parties make sense of the act.

The third and final part that directs the sampling procedure was composed of the possibilities and limitations of the 141 cases. I will return to this issue later in the text.

The process of sampling that emerged from this basis could be compared to a gigantic jig-saw puzzle, whose pieces had to be changed several times in order for them to fit together. My aim was to obtain a balanced sample, taking *degree of seriousness* of the violent behavior, *personal characteristics* of the man and woman, and *the marital life-style* into consideration. As my aim was to capture the distinctive feature of marital woman battering, I wanted to obtain accounts as heterogeneous as possible.

"What is involved when we say what people are doing and why they are doing it?" Burke (1969) asked in his classical discussion of "dramatism". Well-formed stories, Burke proposed, are composed of a pentad with an Act, a Scene, an Agent, an Agency, and a Purpose (Burke 1969). In accordance with these principles, and with my aim to obtain accounts as heterogeneous as possible, I became aware that I needed a group of informants, sufficiently diversified to provide me with narrative accounts of acts of marital woman battering, that together would constitute the "well-formed story" of marital woman battering, including possible variations.

After an initial review of the 141 cases, I divided the material into three groups, covering the range from minor to severe violence. I classified the violent act on the basis of the *degree of seriousness of violent behavior:*

(1) **Minor violence,** such as pushing, grabbing or shoving. Hitting with open hand. Minor injuries to the woman.

(2) **Medium-serious violence,** such as kicking, beating up, and hitting with fists. Medium injuries to the woman.

(3) **Serious violence,** such as serious kicking, serious hitting, and beating up. Attempts at choking. Use of weapon.

I then reviewed the 141 cases once more with the intention of classifying the violent act on the basis of personal characteristics of victim and offender. The material proved to be of limited usefulness in this regard.

Strangely enough, it was not possible to gather the personal characteristics of the men from the records, due to poor documentation. Personal characteristics of the women however were fairly well documented.

In the process of deciding the basis for classifying the women, I was influenced by the previously described endeavors to classify woman battering on the basis of the personal characteristics of the offender and the victim. Battered women have often been described as *fragile,* sometimes as a consequence of the violence (Walker 1979) and sometimes as a contributing factor (Gayford 1979). A fragile woman is one who has severe difficulties in dealing with her life, which are manifested in anxiety, depression, or other psychiatric problems.

In the police records, I found descriptions of women who fitted the above description of a fragile woman. I also found descriptions of women, who, in their contact with the police had appeared capable and decisive, having no serious problems to deal with in their lives, other than with their abusive husbands. In light of the information from the police reports, I characterized these women as *strong.*

My third and final review, concerned the scene of the violent act, the marriage. I found no information on this subject. In order to characterize marital life-style, I used socio-economic status. I then could identify lower-income couples as well as middle- and upper-income couples.

Two of my intended informants declined from participating in the study for the reasons that "it is over now; I don't want to stir it up" and "we already have a counselor; it would be too much". I then chose two new couples. Of the twenty men, two declined personal interviews on the ground that "it is already ruined, why bring it all up again". On the other hand, long telephone conversations with them were possible. Below is how my "puzzle" looked when it was completed:

Introduction of informants

Ulla and Hans A. She is a housewife, he is a plumber with his own company and a good income. Both are about 35 years old and have a six year-old son. Ulla is perceived as fragile, "a little on the nervous side". The more recent battering was very serious. According to the police report, it was pure luck that Ulla survived. They claim not to want to get a divorce.

Sonja and Per B. She is a housewife. He works in the sales department of a big company which implies a high salary with a heavy workload and a lot of traveling. They are about 40 years of age and have a son in school. She has been married previously and has two children from that marriage. Sonja has sought medical treatment several times for anxiety, nervousness, and depression. She has periodically taken psychopharmaceuticals. I label her fragile. She has been subjected to medium-serious violence. Sonja and Per do not want to get divorced.

Katrin and Hector C. She works as an economic assistant at a school, and he drives a bus. Both are in their twenties and have a three year old daughter. K. is perceived as being very capable which is why she is labeled as strong. The violence she was subjected to consisted of shoves, slaps, and having her hair pulled. I label it as minor violence. Katrin wants a divorce. I spoke with Hector by telephone. He is desperate about Katrin wanting to leave him. When he understood that she was serious about this, he left the Greater Stockholm area so that I never met him.

Fathima and Refa D. Both graduated from college in their home country. They moved to Sweden several years prior to our meeting, but have never found work in the fields of their educations. They are in their thirties and have two pre-school sons. Fathima has seen a doctor for her psychosomatic difficulties. She suffers from powerful anxiety attacks. I perceive her as fragile. She has been subjected to medium-serious violence consisting of kicks and slugs. Fathima and Refa want to continue living together.

Irene and Vladimir E. She works as a cashier, but is at present on maternity leave to care for their newborn daughter. He is a carpenter's apprentice, and both are in their twenties. Irene is seen to be very stable. The battering was minor and the couple wants to continue to be together.

Maria and Victor F. Both work as recreational leaders. Maria is about 25 years old, and Victor slightly over 30. They have two young children. Maria is seen as a very competent woman. Victor has battered her seriously. Maria wants to separate.

Marie and Erik G. She works in an office and he is an electrician. Marie wants to separate and has begun divorce proceedings. The battering she has been subjected to is medium-serious. Both are about 35 years old and have four children together. I have spoken with Erik several times on the telephone but have never met him. He explains that his wife has almost left him several times, but realizes now it is for good. He wants to forget everything and look ahead. To participate in the study would mean "stirring up old stuff" which he wants to avoid.

Ruth and Urho H. Both work in the same factory. They are over 40 years old and have two teenage children. Ruth is a small, thin, delicate and fragile woman. Urho has alcohol problems. The battering was medium-serious. Ruth wants a divorce.

Pia and Kjell I. She works as an archivist after long periods of illness and unemployment. Kjell has been on sick leave for a long time after an occupational injury. Both are periodically heavy drinkers. They are about 35 years old and have three school-age children. Kjell has battered Pia seriously. She wants a divorce.

Angela and Pablo J. She is a housewife with three children, and he has had several jobs. Both are just under 30 years old. They are refugees from Latin America. Pablo has battered Angela very seriously. He realizes that he has problems with alcohol; he cannot stop drinking until he is extremely intoxicated. Angela is weak and fragile. They do not want to separate.

Louise and Sven K. Both have college degrees and are about 35 years old with good incomes. They are employed at a large export company. They have a small daughter. Louise is a strong woman. Sven has battered her in a minor way. He wants to separate. They each quickly acquired their own apartment.

Kristina and Carl-Magnus L. Kristina is just under 30 years old and Carl-Magnus is somewhat older. Both have college degrees. Kristina is perceived as a strong woman. The battering was medium-serious. She wants a divorce.

Gunilla and Rolf M. Gunilla works in an office at a government agency and Rolf is a taxi driver. Both are about 40 years old. Over the years, she has suffered from different types of mental insufficiency. Gunilla has a child from a previous marriage and two children with Rolf. The battering was minor to medium-serious. She wants a divorce.

Viveka and Adam N. She has been on sick leave for a long time due to an occupational injury. She is now attending a retraining course. She has problems with substance abuse. Adam is a messenger. Viveka has children from a previous marriage. Both are about 35 years old. The battering was medium-serious and they want to continue as a couple.

Susanne and Paul O. She is a nurse's assistant and he is a clerk. Both are almost 40 years old and have three children together. Susanne has substance abuse problems and is often depressed and worried. The battering was serious, but they want to continue together.

Nina and Fredrik P. Nina works as a secretary in a large company. Fredrik is an assistant manager and earns a good income. Nina is just 30 years and Fredrik some years older. They have a five-year old daughter together. Nina had mental problems during her childhood and still does. Fredrik has battered her medium-seriously. They want to continue together.

Lisa and Ismeth Q. Lisa is a nurse, a very competent woman with a responsible job. Ismeth is a waiter, but has also engaged in some business. Both are about 35 years old and have a daughter of pre-school age. Lisa has been very seriously battered and has obtained a divorce.

Annika and Mats R. Both are about 20 years old. She is working on a college degree and is seen as very competent. He is working as a craftsman. They have no children. The battering was medium-serious. They want to continue together.

Lena and Birger S. Lena works as a nurse. She has previously had mental problems of various types, but feels better now. Birger is a painter with alcohol problems. They have a small daughter together. He is about 30 and she is five years older. The battering was medium-serious and they want to continue together.

Pirjo and Ove T. She is a housewife and he is a businessman with a high income. She is about 25 years old and he is ten years older. They have a son together. She is a strong woman who has been medium-seriously battered. She wants a divorce.

What is a Swedish marriage?

A Swedish poet once wrote something along the lines of "Swedish gooseberries only in Sweden are found". This expression has been widely quoted and has been used to describe the supremacy of Sweden and the benefits that Sweden offers.

As recently as a half century ago, Sweden was fairly isolated from the world. At the end of the 1800s and the beginning of the 1900s, immigration was quite limited in contrast to the widespread emigration. Then came the two world wars and the closing of borders. It was relatively easy at that time to define what a "Swedish gooseberry" was.

Circumstances have changed. Now, in the 1990s, the world is pressing in from all directions. It is no longer possible to be certain about what type of berry a "Swedish gooseberry" is. Our Swedish King's ancestors immigrated from France during the early 1800s and our queen was born in Germany and raised in Brazil; thus, there is also reason to question just what a Swedish marriage is.

The women and men in three of my informant couples were both born outside of the Nordic countries, and two of the couples were citizens of another Nordic country. In three of the couples, the men were non-Nordic, and one man was born in Sweden of parents from a non-Nordic country. According to prevailing terminology, these couples would be classified as "immigrant marriages" or "mixed marriages".

Examining the class composition of the couples results in another picture. In their country of origin, a couple such as Fathima and Refa D. belonged to an intellectual upwardly mobile middle class. He belonged to an ethnic minority in their country of origin, but she did not. Her father was a successful business executive, and her brothers were following in his footsteps. Fathima and Refa's basic values were largely similar to those of two other informant couples with higher education and whose families had lived in Sweden for generations. Furthermore, it can be assumed that the three hard-working men with high incomes and wives who did not work away from home also have similar values, despite the fact that only two of them have a completely Swedish background. The same probably also applies to the three well-educated women in my informant group despite the fact that they as well do not have the same nationality of origin.

In a period of social and national mobility, it is not especially useful to continue to view nation states and societies as isolated entities or to divide Sweden into "Swedes" and "immigrants", or to use concepts such as "immigrant marriage" or "mixed marriage". It is my contention that what constitutes the cultural domicile of a marriage is not primarily the country of origin of the couple. The maritally constituting rules are culturally determined at a deeper level. A man and a woman who live in a marital relationship must take into consideration those rules which reflect the norms and conceptions of how a marriage ought to be. Moving to another country implies an encounter with a new culture, with new rules which reflect norms and conceptions about marriage. Such an encounter may imply a confirmation of, or a challenge to, something previously assumed. A change leads to the coming of something new.

What my informants all have in common, besides being domiciled in Sweden, is that they speak good Swedish and that they work and operate in Sweden. In addition, all of the men have repeatedly battered their wives. Some of the men who had immigrated to Sweden also battered their wives in their countries of origin, and others had battered them only in Sweden. A Swedish-born plumber, an exiled freedom fighter who struggled against fascism in his country of origin, a Swedish-born man on a disability pension, and a businessman born in one of our neighboring countries all have wife battering in common.

What my informant couples also have in common is that they embrace the idea of *romantic love* as the base for a marriage. In Western culture, the concept of "romantic love" gradually has come to contain intense claims for personal fulfillment and wishes for reconciliation and belongingness. By its promises of sexual gratification, reproduction and unity, the marital way of life here plays an important role in the carrying out of this idea. Thus, in a society organized along patriarchal lines as our Western society's, there are endless examples of how these promises are not fulfilled. Marriages can be turned into battlefields, with the exercise of a rigid pattern of dominance and subordination first on the agenda. Nevertheless, patriarchy depends upon female participation. In order to understand the driving forces behind this participation of women, one must take into account the female benefits like maintenance, protection and social status, that might derive from the patriarchal arrangement. One also must take into account the difficulties she will be faced with in her efforts to attain the above mentioned benefits on her own.

Throughout history we have witnessed endless variations of the theme "man offers protection and social status to a women in exchange for access to her body, as well as access to her care for him and their children". There have also been endless examples of his use of force in order to obtain what could be taken by force, such as access to her body, in case she has denied him access voluntarily. This creates a paradoxical situation: the idea of "romantic love" does not know of any violence, still, it has been shaped in a culture containing men's violent actions towards women. The ideal for the masculine man in the context of "romantic love" will hardly contain much of violent action either, but rather his belief of being a powerful, energetic and supportive person, able to maintain his family. This ideal presents the woman with the complementary character, one that confirms his position and praises his capacity for maintenance. To my understanding, masculinity, as we in a Western cultural context understand its basic feature, would in all probability not be conceivable without the woman as a complementary person.

For her confirmation to be of any credibility and value, she must be somebody and add something to his being, and take the complementary position. As the complementary character, she could either be idealized and treated with respect, or be nobody and be belittled and used. The notion of "romantic love" as the ideal base for marital life in a patriarchal society will provide the background for all my informant couples' marriages.

Gaining access to information

The *act of interviewing* holds a prominent place in my study. In my view, the research act first comes alive during the interview when the researcher is forced to confront the informants on a direct, face-to-face level. The process of interviewing in this study lasted over a two-year period with recurrent interviews, with the woman or the man separately or the couple jointly. My first encounter with the informants took place shortly after the latest defined violent incident. It was facilitated by my continuous contact with the police and social welfare authorities during the period of data collection. As soon as I had selected a couple, the social worker or supervisor in question told the woman about me and my work, and asked if it was all right for me to call her. Two out of twenty replied negatively, after which I selected two other women.

During the initial telephone call, I introduced myself and my study, and set up a time for an initial interview with the woman. In addition, I discussed the matter of contacting her husband in order to set up an initial interview with him. The most common response by the women was that their husbands surely needed to talk to someone, but they were far too scared to do so. I was encouraged either to call or write to the husbands, or both, or the woman agreed to do this for me.

The first contact was planned as soon after the most recent incident of battering as possible. For guidelines here, I used Walker's (1979) description of marital woman battering as an event with three distinct phases: the tension building phase; the explosion or acute battering incident; and the calm and loving respite (Walker 1979 p. 55). During the tension building phase, the woman concentrates on avoiding the violence, and this often means having no contact outside the couple which would arouse the man's anger. The calm and loving respite phase is characterized by the husband being contrite and tender. Both parties' energies are devoted to the marriage and to making everything good again. There is not much chance that either of the parties would be willing to share these experiences with an outside researcher during this phase. It is during the explosive phase that the need for contact with the outside world and the desire for communication with others about what has happened are the strongest.

Even at the most correctly chosen point in time, questioning an informant about phenomena considered to be social problems is a demanding task. Not least of all is this the case in a study about an act of questionable morality where the involved actors are to serve as informants. In order to accept an invitation to participate in such studies, the informants must feel a strong affinity for the project. Obtaining the women's participation was fairly easy. In general they sympathized with the purpose of my work and their need to talk seemed endless.

The men, on the other hand, reacted differently. In order to ensure their participation, considerable efforts were necessary. The men were hesitant about my work and did not expect anything positive from it. Instead, they anticipated a great deal of discomfort from participation. Until I had shown a willingness to listen with an open mind to *their* story, no interview could take place. My view of the research act as a joint enterprise between researcher and informants was shown to be ethically imperative and essential to the realization of the research activity.

Due to the fact that I was exploring a morally questionable human act, these encounters were not entirely uncomplicated for me either. Contact with a person under attack, as with a battered woman, may be difficult as it arouses feelings of powerlessness and anger in the empathetic interviewer as well. Nor is meeting the woman unproblematic since sympathies so unambiguously lie with her – she is the good and afflicted one. The difficulties lie in attempting to see her as a whole person and to discover darker, more forbidding shadows intertwined with the good.

The majority of the individual interviews with the husbands were conducted by a male colleague. The interviews with a husband, the perpetrator of violence, were complicated in another way than those with the woman. For an empathetic interviewer to come close to a battering man means coming in contact with his or her own aggressive sides, his or her own repressive and brutally controlling sides, and may lead to reflections about his or her own means of exercising power. My male colleague, who was an experienced interviewer, found it difficult to listen to accounts of how members of his own sex inflicted suffering on women. It might have been tempting for him to ignore the man's violence and seek for other aspects of his character, such as vulnerability and powerlessness, and identify with these traits instead. Or he could have avoided the problem by simply refusing to become especially close to the subject and by shutting out his story.

If a researcher's capacity for empathy is not maintained, the encounter with an informant could be severely damaged, and the possibilities of gaining access to, in this case, the couple's narratives would be considerably reduced. There was an additional difficulty for me as a woman in the first interview with the husband: My own fear and insecurity, coming face-to-face with a man with well-documented violent tendencies towards women. I remember one encounter that illustrates my fear, and the way in which I dealt with it.

An initial encounter

After having conducted the initial interview with one of my female informants, we agreed that she would soon thereafter inform her husband about me and my research project. Weeks passed without any action from her side. Finally, she called and asked me to come to her home to discuss the matter once more. When I arrived at her house at the agreed time, the door was opened by her husband. He was large and stocky, dressed in jeans and a sleeveless T-shirt that revealed well-developed arm muscles. I perceived him as threatening, which undoubtedly showed in my facial expression. I stepped backwards. In the hall behind the man, I saw the woman who was small and delicate and almost hidden behind him. "I haven't said anything; I thought it was better if you did it yourself", she said, a remark that caused the man to look, if possible, even angrier. I felt very small and no research method whatsoever could help me in that moment as to how I should react. The only guidelines that came to mind were those I learned from my parents, so I stuck out my hand to shake his and said "Good evening". The man shook my hand and when I felt how sweaty it was, I understood that he was afraid. I suddenly felt calm. I gave him my name, apologized for disturbing them at home, and suggested that we go into the hallway for a few minutes so that I could explain what I wanted. I was shown in, and became fully aware of how generous it was of him to let me in. A Swedish man's home is his castle, and it was I who had violated the privacy of their home and had forced my way in.

I gave a brief introduction of myself. He watched me skeptically. I told him that I had met several men in similar situations as his – men with police reports hanging over their heads – and told him that these other men were relieved to have a chance to talk about these things – as strange as that may sound. I told him that I wanted to listen to his and his wife's experiences, since they had experienced things of great interest to many people. The man started seeming curious. I thanked him for letting me present my request, and started backing out towards the door. He conferred briefly with his wife and asked me to come back in. I replied, "A half an hour in that case, since I do not want to disturb you any longer than that", to which they agreed.

With few exceptions, the interviews took place in the informants' homes and were conducted within strict frameworks of time and focus. This was especially important during the joint interviews, where the emotional temperature sometimes rose to such a pitch that a violent outburst seemed imminent. The joint interviews were conducted by me and my male colleague, and we never allowed the emotional temperature to rise to a dangerous level. We interrupted the brewing fight by turning to each of the parties individually and trying to illuminate the impending violent situation. This procedure led to the identification of crucial areas of my informants' marital lives. It provided us all, informants as well as researchers, with information about these areas and the feelings associated with them. A hope for change was presupposed in this procedure; we perceived a risk for a violent incident to break out, but we also experienced the prevention of violent outbursts.

Couple	Woman	Man	Joint	
A	2	1	7	
B	2	1	2	
C	2	tel.	–	
D	3	2	2	
E	2	1	2	
F	3	2	3	
G	4	tel.	–	
H	3	2	1	
I	2	2	7	
J	2	1	1	
K	3	3	3	
L	2	2	2	
M	4	2	4	
N	3	1	2	
O	2	2	1	
P	2	1	8	
Q	12	1	–	
R	2	2	7	
S	4	2	1	
T	2	3	2	
Total	**59**	**30**	**54**	**143**

Table 3:3 Number of interviews.

Over a two-year period, 143 personal interviews were conducted, 30 of which were with men and 59 with women separately, and 54 with the couples together. These interviews lasted 45–60 minutes, and 60–90 minutes, respectively. Two of the men refused any face-to-face interviewing, but accepted being interviewed by telephone. (Table 3:3) In addition, numerous and lengthy complementary telephone conversations were held. The interviews were recorded and typed. The material covers a total of about 1,600 pages of written text.

Table 3:3 reflects a conscious and controlled way of conducting the interviews, as well as the uncontrolled outcome of this strategy. The underlying idea of the way of conducting the interviews was my assumption that it would be easier to obtain a valid and detailed account of what had happened if the informants themselves were able to determine the external conditions for the interview as well as its form, and further, to have the possibility to influence the choice of interview topics. In this respect my research approach has a close kinship to feminist research. (For a presentation of feminist research approach, see further Haavind 1987; Kelly 1988; Yllö and Bograd 1988.) I consider this idea to be proven successful. However, it carried some uncontrolled consequences. There are some interviews missing, and there is a considerable range of variation in the frequency of interviews among the informants. I could have decided to "push" harder, but in line with the general idea that directed my way of conducting the interviews, I refrained from it. The "high-frequency" couples then made considerable contributions to my study, contributions that were used as such, as well as "suggestion-givers" to areas of special interest that were used in the interviews with the "low-frequency" couples to make them as rewarding as possible. What the interviews had in common, however, was that they all dealt with the violent incident.

Interviewing as a discourse between speakers

Interviews hold a prominent place among research methods in my study, and in social science in general. The term *interview* generally refers to a specialized pattern of verbal interaction in which the role relationship of interviewer and respondent is highly specialized. This makes interviews a *behavioral* rather than a *linguistic* event, and the standard conception of interviewing as behavior is to a great extent based on the stimulus-response paradigm of the experimental laboratory (Mishler 1986).

Prior to our first meeting, one of my male informants told me during a telephone conversation:

> Yeah, of course I'll be part of your study. I have been through a lot, I really have. If you think that someone else can be helped by this, then it is good. But I am not at all sure that you will get anything out of this. The fact is that I don't *know* anything about what happened. (Hans A, telephone call).

What this man is describing is something he has in common with most of my informants. He has been through "a lot", but about what happened he is very unclear. The events seem taken out of context with no internal relationship. He himself is a walking question mark and is being honest when he claims he knows nothing.

In the initial phase of interviewing, the women suffered from feelings of anxiety and fear. They too had a very hazy picture of what had happened, since the course of events were associated with fear and unsuccessful attempts at self-protection.

Events of this kind are not easy to reconstruct. Large portions of the story are lacking, as is the logic that keeps the story running. When I met my informants, I felt that one of my primary responsibilities was to help them reconsider the violent events and open up access to their own story. I wanted my informants to describe the affective, cognitive, and evaluative meanings they attached to the events, as well as their different kinds of involvement.

If I had to identify a single factor which was significant for being successful in gaining access to couples' narratives of marital violence, I would mention my growing insight that *the process of interviewing can be a jointly conducted enterprise between interviewer and interviewee.* (See further Bruner 1990; Kohler Riessman 1990; Mishler 1991). Accordingly, I allowed the informant interviewees to actively shape and form the interviews together with me in a joint process.

In such a process, the concepts of *question* and *answer* are to be thought of as a part of a circular process, with my informants and I trying to make continuing sense of what we were talking about. This way of conducting interviews differs from standard interviewing, according to which a question which has a predetermined meaning serves as a stimulus and is intended to elicit a certain response (Mishler 1991). If I had conducted my interviews along those lines, I would most likely have faced considerable difficulties, for example, in confronting the above quoted man's notion of "not knowing anything about what had happened". By transforming my efforts to obtain answers into a joint enterprise between my informants and myself, I was able to overcome these difficulties.

When taking the initiative in an exchange of statements, I was guided by my view of woman battering within the marriage as a marital act, and in accordance with my way of conceptualizing "the marriage". In the example below, taken from an initial interview with Irene E, a young woman of 23, my questions and her answers intertwine, gradually shaping her view of herself and her life project:

> I: If you were to describe yourself very briefly for me, who has never met you before, what would you say?
> IP: Oh...I don't know...yeah, I am rather shy. So I am rather unsure of myself. I am pretty calm. I don't know what more to say.
> I: In what ways are you unsure of yourself?
> IP: Well, for example, if I am on the subway...and someone starts staring at me a little too long...I get embarrassed...I start thinking, 'What do I do now?'

At times in the subsequent interviews, she took the initiative, as in the example below. The pattern of intertwining questions and answers is retained:

> IP: What I think about most of the time is the future. Worrying about this trial is just starting.

I: What are you afraid of...if you can tell me about that?

IP: (sighs deeply)...That I won't be able to get through it....

I: What does get through it mean?

IP: That I won't fall completely apart...Everything is turned upside down for me right now...you know, it's like watching an old movie. I go over about everything I've been through these past years...just the fact that I once trusted him.

The following questions were directed to the woman and the man in the initial, individually conducted interviews:

Can you tell me what happened? How did it begin...then what happened...how did it end...then what happened...is this the way it usually happens?

How would you describe yourself briefly to an outsider like me?

How would you describe your husband/wife to an outsider like me?

When your husband/wife is interviewed, how do you think he/she is going to describe himself/herself?

When your husband/wife is interviewed, how do you think he/she is going to describe you?

What would be necessary to put a stop to the violent incidents?

The first five of these questions invited reflection. The last question encouraged the interviewee to discuss anticipated future-assigned tasks in regard to the marital violence. This kind of framework provided an opportunity to discuss the violence in a context which encompassed the possibility for change. In my view, this frame was essential for gaining access to my informants' accounts of the violent incidents. By means of this procedure, these histories, which contained people's deepest and darkest secrets, could be narrated from a perspective which allowed hope for change.

The initial phase of interviewing was followed by a second phase of individual or joint interviews. The answers to the question "What would be necessary to put a stop to the violent incidents?" served as a transition to the second interview phase. The answers given to that question formed the main issue taken up during the subsequent interview phase.

Underlying the design of the second interview round with topics selected by the informants themselves was my assumption that it would be easier to obtain a valid and credible story if the informants were able themselves to determine the content of the interviews. In similar fashion, I allowed the informants to determine whether the second round of interviews would be separate or joint. The majority of the couples chose the joint interview alternative.

One problem arising from this working method was that the topic to be discussed during the second round of interviews was selected in the individual interviews, whereas the second interview was often a joint interview. Frequently the man and the woman in the same couple chose completely antagonistic topics to be discussed.

In the case of one couple, the woman wanted to separate and wanted the second round of interviews to take up this fact, whereas the man was terrified even to think about separation and did not want to discuss it at all. Both described their joint life as "a big mess". It was this "mess" that eventually served as the common denominator for the two parties, and which eventually became the topic for the second round of interviews. This theme was formulated as "an attempt to create order and clarity about what had happened". Parenthetically, the dialogue with this couple ended with the man deciding to ensure that they got a divorce (Gunilla and Rolf M).

It was simpler with another couple where both the man's and woman's energies were focused on the experience of loss of control and powerlessness in the battering situation. Both wanted the relationship to continue; both were terrified that the battering would recur. In the second round of interviews, we focused on feelings of powerlessness and loss of control and the battering situation was charted in minute detail as was the context in which it had occurred (Ulla and Hans A).

The ranking order of the issues chosen, according to an estimation of the frequency of occurrence, is as follows:

He must stop hitting me.

She has to calm down.

I want a divorce.

We have to understand what happens when we start arguing, so that it doesn't end up in violence.

He has to understand me better.

I want her back. It is a big mess – we have to sort it out.

We have to learn to talk to each other.

Everything needs to be discussed – here we need someone with a big heart.

She has to stop drinking so much.

The second interview phase thus consisted of a *topic interview,* where the interviewees used my question as a basis for articulating the issue they felt was most relevant. The detailed content of the various interviews diverged, whereas the general content was more uniform. Regardless of the topic that served as the point of departure for the separate interviews, the violent event was the focus of all of the interviews.

Despite the fact that every interview with this design had a unique format, the final results display more similarities than dissimilarities. In all interviews, the violent event was the focus, even if the informants describe it from divergent perspectives and with emphasis on different aspects.

Combining and confronting accounts of violence

The design of my study and my conceptualization of the act of interviewing are both characterized by my conviction that what one can expect as a researcher who asks people to discuss sensitive and painful events are accounts filled with contradictions and omitted sequences. For an outsider to partake of the story, I believe that it is necessary to allow it to evolve as a discourse between informant and interviewer. I will further explore here the implications of this proposition. I will show how a longitudinal study is preferable to a cross-sectional study due to the fact that it provides the opportunity to *combine* and *confront* the stories.

It is impossible to say everything on one occasion. The informants' accounts are thus time-specific. During an interview immediately following the violent event, the feelings are intense; during a later interview, the story may be characterized by reconciliation; and a third interview may be filled with grief and hopelessness. It is impossible to avoid time-specific accounts, but it is possible to make them fuller by combining the stories told during different interview sessions.

One further possibility for obtaining a full account is to confront the other with the different stories. A simple example is the men's and the women's individual accounts about what had happened. These stories were basically different, which is why the parties experienced the events from fundamentally different perspectives. Consistently, the woman's stories were more detailed than those of the men who were more reticent. Pointing this out to the man in several cases led him to elaborate with more details.

A more complicated example concerns one of my female informants. During the initial interview, she gave an account of battering that she did not perceive as particularly serious:

> We had a big fight and I ran up to the bedroom. He ran after me and slugged me. (Ulla A, individual interview)

After this battering incident, Ulla A was compelled to go to the hospital and the event was reported to the police. Police reports and physical reports described an aggravated assault leading to injuries which could have cost Ulla her life. Her husband's account resembled the police's, but Ulla persisted in her account when she was confronted with the considerable discrepancy in the accounts. The dialogue that followed about this discrepancy resulted in Ulla's recalling more and more from her childhood. In light of this, her account became easier to understand. Earlier in life, she had been subjected to repeated violence from her father, had learned to keep it inside, and had cut off her feelings of hate and denial; she had later decided that the battering was not of much consequence. Challenges of her account led to that one important topic rising to the surface, namely, the correlation between prior and present experiences of violence.

On another occasion, I confronted a man with his way of accounting for the violent act. This man often returned to a favorite description:

> **IP:** You see, in our heads there is a place with two poles. There has to be a certain distance between them. When you get angry, you get close to one of the poles. In my head, the poles are too close together, so that when I get angry, they crash into each other. I can see on your face that you don't believe me, but it is in fact true. A doctor himself told me this. I think it was caused by a motorcycle accident I was in.
> **I:** How can you tell when this happens?
> **IP:** I simply get a total blackout. I get mad and then PANG, it crashes and I am not aware of anything for a long time. When I come to again, I have often done something violent. Hit Pia or trashed the apartment.
> **I:** Then it must be unbelievable luck that Pia is still alive.
> **IP:** What do you mean?
> **I:** I mean that when you get mad at her and it short-circuits in your head, your body takes on a life of its own and becomes violent. It is lucky that you haven't stuck the bread knife in her, or scissors, or hit her even worse than you have.
> **IP:** Are you crazy or something?!! Do you think that I could do such a thing. I would never be able to hurt her that bad! (Kjell I, joint interview)

After being confronted in this way, Kjell I's account became more detailed. Moreover, my behavior led to the central topic of analysis being exposed, namely, the special *rhetoric of exculpation* used by both men and women for describing the violent event. I will return to this in a later chapter.

I came into close contact with my informants' lives following one of the man's violent outbursts. When I pose the question, "Can you tell me what happened?", most of the informants' responses referred to the most recent violent incident. As the interview process proceeded however, the informants' shift over to descriptions of a *typical incident:* "It usually begins with....and so on".

When I call my study a longitudinal study, it is this "typical" nature of the violent incident that is referred to. This incident and my informants' processing of it are followed through their narratives. Two cases of violence or imminent violence occurred during the study period. Thus, there is no constant flow of violent incidents.

Narratives of violence

By asking questions such as "How did it begin?" and "Then what happened?", I invited my informants to produce a *narrative account of personal experience.* The transformation of experience into a narrative is a prototypic form of talk that we acquire as children and a form of talk we use to structure our own experience to make sense of what happens to us, as well as to transmit our personal experiences to others (Mishler 1991; Bruner 1990; Kohler Riessman 1990). *Temporality* is usually seen as the defining characteristic of a narrative, that is to say, the events are told in the order in which they are believed to have unfolded in actual life. A traditional narrative (Ong 1982) contains a beginning, a middle and an end, as the logic that keeps the story running. My informants shaped their narratives as dramas in three parts, beginning with a *pre-history,* progressing through the *violent incident,* and ending in the *aftermath.*

In relation to that structure, the men and women among my informants shaped their narratives somewhat differently. The women mainly concentrated on the middle of the narrative, the violent incident itself, and on their strong feelings of powerlessness, fear, and anger that the man's violence had elicited. The men were not as preoccupied with the violent incident, as with the consequences of the violence. They talked about their fear of the legal process that could be triggered if their wives decided to report what they had done, and they talked about their fear of being condemned by their fellow beings. The men's narratives thus began in the aftermath phase. They proceeded to discuss the argument that had preceded the outbreak of violence in the overwhelming majority of cases, while the women were occupied with the violent incident. Had I not pushed them to continue the narratives by filling in what they had omitted, they would not in all probability have done so.

What I was dealing with here were *reported events,* not observations of the events themselves. Without any ambition to approach the complexity of the relationship between reality and reported reality in considerable detail, I will make here some notes on the subject.

Goffman (1974) conveys a view of the many-sided relationship between reality and reports of reality, between action in the world and the speech about that action. On the one hand, Goffman states, reports of events are framed in ways that are highly conventionalized. On the other hand, behavior itself incorporates imitations and replayings, strips derived from those conventional representations. Consequently, narrative accounts are not unreal accounts in the sense of being unrelated to reality. They are *framed accounts,* they are transformations of reality, and with proper attention to the frames and the rules of transformation, we can begin to reconstitute their relations to the wider frames outside of the narrative context (Goffman 1974; pp. 560–562; Labov 1982).

In this view, it is essential to pay attention to and expose the kind of rhetoric that is used for describing the violent event. This kind of speech reflects the violent actions, as well as the cultural norms encompassing them.

For the purpose of my study, that is, to chart out the husband's and the wife's means of constructing and understanding the violent events, it has been fundamentally important to gain access to the parties' narrative accounts of what happened. Observations of the events had not, irrespective of the ethical aspects, for three main reasons been satisfactory.

The event I have been studying is a *repeated* action. When the parties describe a specific event, the event is unique in itself; at the same time it is a recurring type of event. In order to understand marital violence, this recurring nature is of central importance. Only the parties involved have had this experience, and not any casual observer.

The event I have studied is an *undesirable* event; it is not an event that is automatically assumed to be part of a marriage. This undesirability, while the parties are part of what is happening, is not easily observed by means of direct observation. It is something that first and foremost must be described by the parties involved.

The events I have studied are events where two people find

themselves in *opposition* to each other. Such an event cannot be described as *one* event. On the contrary, it is an inherent feature that such an event involves two separate histories, two separate ways of accounting for, pondering over, and explaining it. An observer in all likelihood perceives such an event as one event. For the interviewer, it quickly becomes clear that it is a matter of two stories that do not necessarily agree with or even resemble each other.

Writing people's narratives into a text of social science

Initially, I referred to the conceptualization of the research act as "those endeavors of a researcher to take her or him from theory to methods, to the empirical world and back again" (Denzin 1978 p. ix). In my study, this has meant moving from the theoretical work of conceptualizing woman battering within the marriage as a marital act, towards the empirical world of the batterer's and battered's narrative accounts of the event and then back again to theory, thus jumping from the narratives of men's and women's experiences located in the particular context of their lives, to the objectified non-personal forms of knowing and reasoning in a scientific text. This process represents the analytical phase of the research act.

In an article concerning women's studies, Smith (1991) argues for the existence of a contradiction between women's experiences and texts written in the context of standard sociological discourse. She contends that a break has occurred between the embodied subject, situated in the particular local sites, and the subject in a textually mediated discourse of sociology. She argues in favor of a sociology which adopts conventions for writing texts that take a standpoint in women's actual experiences. A sociology beginning here, Smith proposes, would explore the actual relations organizing and determining people's lives and discover for us the realities of what is going on and of the relations that connect and separate us (Smith 1991).

When Smith pleads for a text that speaks from the informant's experiences, her position on the relation between theory and empirical research is similar to that of Glaser and Strauss in their work on "grounded theory". The three of them reject a social science which is solely occupied with verifying either "grand theory" or an ideological position. Glaser and Strauss argue for the "release of energies for theorizing that are now frozen by the undue emphasis on verification" (Glaser and Strauss 1979 p.viii). Smith's arguments advocate more a "release" of the female informant and her retention as subject in the text, and not being reduced or imprisoned by categories like "interpersonal relations", "socialization", "psychosocial processes of the family" and the like, for describing her experiences. According to Smith, this kind of release is more a question of "the discovery of a language" - to describe, define, and clarify the women's experiences – than a question of "the discovery of theory".

But texts are not solely intermediaries of experience. Texts are also organizers of our relations as readers with that which is written. This could be illustrated by our differing relationships to the battered woman, depending on whether she is described as a masochist or as a sister in a patriarchal society. A masochist is a negatively viewed person, a sister is the opposite. The latter is someone we would like to know, and can identify with. Similar to the description of a woman as a "masochist", though, the word "sister" contains a knowledge emanating from an outside position. In the first case, the appealed observer's attempt to understand is embedded in the text; in the second, an empathetic woman seems to be present.

During the leap from collecting narratives of people's experiences to the analysis of these narratives, I have tried to maintain the subjects' accounts as the basic unit of research. I rejected the position of "being on the outside looking in". An outside position would have implied the presence of interpretative frameworks, such as individually-oriented psychological perspectives, or family-oriented systems theory. I rejected this at the very beginning of my study, and during the collection of data I made extensive efforts to retain my autonomy, in a theoretical and ideological sense of the word. I did not want to be blinded, and would not let the encounter with my informants be determined by general theories. My main interest concerned the endeavor of the husband and wife, as batterer and battered, to make sense of what had happened. The analytical approach I used concerned the *content* of their accounts, as well as the *form* and *the missing parts of these accounts*. In other words, what they told, how they told it, and what they did not tell.

Exploring narrative accounts

Well-formed stories, as Burke pointed out in his work on dramatism, are composed of a pentad of act, agent, scene, agency, and purpose. Any complete statement about motive will offer some kind of answer to these five questions: What was done (Act), when or where it was done (Scene), who did it (Agent), how he did it (Agency), and why (Purpose)? (Burke 1969).

For the analysis of the content of the narrative accounts, Burke's conceptualization of a story served well as a guide. I will give an example:

> It was just 'stop it, stop talking shit'. Like, I just didn't want to hear any more. I had heard enough. But I never wanted to hurt her. She means too much to me for that. This hitting stuff is just a warning. Otherwise, I could just as well take a pistol and shoot her. I know I am hard-handed. She says so too. But I'm not hard on purpose. I am also soft. She admits that. But women are different from men. Women are psychologically stronger, they say. I just react: 'Now, damnit. You are going to keep quiet. Don't say another fucking word.' I don't say 'now you are going to get it so you die.' It is not like that. (Vladimir E, individual interview)

When I manipulated the account in order to impute Burke's concepts, the result was as follows:

> In the living-room of their joint home (Scene), the husband (Agent) hits (Agency) his wife (Counter-agent) in order (Purpose) to stop her from talking (Act).

I found the dramatic pentad most useful while exploring the pre-history and the violent incident. For the analytical work concerning the aftermath I developed a somewhat different approach. I will come back to this in chapter 7.

The thesis I put forward during the analytical work of this study is, that what *has not* been talked about in people's narratives is as important as that which *has* been talked about. In the following chapters, you will find some traces of my deconstructive reading of the informants' accounts as well as of my constructive reading.

A deconstructive reading relies on gaps in consistency and contradictions in the text, and even on metaphorical associations for revealing meanings present in the text but outside any immediate level of awareness. This kind of reading links my analytical work with my work as an interviewer. My task as an interviewer to listen and respond to the informants' narrative accounts is very much akin to a deconstructive reading of the narratives.

A note on the effects of the research

The essence of the interviewing technique I have used is to be found in the joint construction of meaning by my informants and me. In such a procedure, a narrative is never concluded, but is always subjected to reconstruction and reinterpretation. Due to this continuous reinterpretation, participation in this kind of study *implies change.*

I was able to witness the unfolding of many dramatic reinterpretations during my study. One of them concerned a female informant. When I asked her during our first encounter to describe her husband and herself, she used negative terms about herself but enthusiastic terms about her husband. The next time I met her, she was furious:

> After you left, I almost threw up. Listening to myself talking sweet about him. This really makes me sick. The truth is that I am finished with him. People can think whatever they want. I don't give a damn. Do you know what happened? He started to drink again. And of course, lots of people come running to his aid: his physician, his AA mates, his colleagues. I get sick, I really do. Everybody takes his side; nobody, and I mean nobody, is siding with me and my son. And I am just another idiot in his fan-club, praising him. Oh my God! (Lena S, individual interview)

In addition to reaching this conclusion, this woman arranged for an extra place for her husband to live, and made it a condition for the continued marriage that he moved there during times of trouble.

A second, not less dramatic reconstruction, concerned one of the men. During a joint interview, I, my male colleague, and his wife, were talking. The man was gazing out the window, silently. Suddenly he turned towards us:

> You may get the impression I'm not interested. That is not the case. On the contrary, I am listening to every word. You see, I also have had the answers to the questions you are asking my wife. But I never had the questions. And these questions...I have searched for them my whole life. (Rolf M, joint interview)

The fact that the events to be discussed were morally questionable, was a central determinant of my encounters with the informants. People involved in such acts usually keep these experiences secret, and thereby deprive themselves of the opportunity to communicate about these acts with other people. The experiences of violence then remain secret memories, expunged from the life-histories of those involved. The experiences are removed from their context and remain isolated even, or maybe especially, when they are of major significance. The process of interviewing itself, and the interaction between the researcher and the informant to some degree put words to the hidden memories and make sense of them, a process which can be interpreted by the parties as both positive and negative.

The act of research – a summary

This study concerns how husbands and wives make sense of violent action within their marriages. The group of informants consists of cases that were defined over the course of one year by the police and the social authorities in a Stockholm suburb as "woman battering". Altogether, this group included 141 cases. Some basic data on the battering files were collected about this group.

Among the 141 cases, I selected a group of twenty couples. Over a two-year period, 143 personal interviews were conducted, 30 of which were with the men and 59 with the women separately, and 54 with the couples together. In a jointly constructed process between interviewer and interviewees, the violent events were identified and described, as to how they were interpreted, explained, and justified by those involved.

Over the years, I developed a feminist research approach that allowed me insight into the points of view of the women as well as of the men I studied. It made it possible for me to share my informants' social knowledge of marital woman battering. By using this approach, I gained access to their statements or narrative accounts of the violent acts, including their explanations for them.

4

The Pre-history

Introduction

> When I think about how it all started...it's kind of embarrassing...we were arguing over which channel we were going to watch... such nonsense. You may not believe that it's possible to fight about TV programs. It can turn into a huge brawl. Even I don't really understand it. A gigantic fight. When I think that I almost got killed for a television program. Good God! (Ulla A, individual interview)

"How did it begin?" was one of the questions posed early in my interviews. Eighteen of the couples agreed with Ulla A's interpretation above that it all started with reciprocal verbal aggressive behavior concerning a commonplace issue, trivial enough to be embarrassing to recall. The male and female informants were remarkably agreed on this point. The events however were described somewhat differently from couple to couple: as a quarrel, an argument, or a verbal fight.

Two of my informant couples made no mention of any kind of verbal aggressive behavior as the precursor to the violent event. The man in one of these couples identified his desire for revenge as the force which drove him to commit a severe act of violence. It was his perception that his wife had subjected him to pain, unfair treatment, and degradation during their marriage to such an extent that he felt justified in exacting vengeance upon her. The woman viewed the attack on her as totally incomprehensible; she was deeply shocked and extremely frightened.

Both parties in the second of the two couples viewed their imminent divorce as the decisive situational factor leading to the violent outburst. Powerful feelings of anger, abandonment, and the husband's attempt to compel his wife to remain in the marriage by means of violence, characterize the pre-history to the violent act for this couple.

In this chapter, the narrative accounts of these three different kinds of pre-histories will be examined. The focus will be on accounts of the most frequently occurring kind of pre-history, or that which is referred to by the informants as a verbal fight, an argument, or a quarrel. The form and procedures used by the couples to construct this act will be described.

The initial phase of the verbal aggressive act

"Money, sex, children, communication – this is the stuff life is made of", states family therapist Goldberg (1982) in an article about family conflict. He continues: "Certainly husbands and wives will be involved with these matters and will find cause for complaints about them" (Goldberg 1982). In their study of violence in the American family, Straus et al.(1980) mentioned five issues which often lead to conflict: money, children, housekeeping, social activities, and sex (Straus et al. 1980). Stets (1990) discusses verbal aggression in marriage, concluding that it is often related to physical aggression.

According to my informants, the first step in the verbal aggressive episode was an utterance about a commonplace issue, constructed as an *opposition* in regard to the issue in question.

The concept of opposition originates from the research tradition within linguistics and social psychology where disputes are studied as speech events. the analytic unit in focus, the dispute, is divided into three utterances or phases: the antecedent event, the opposition, and the reaction to that opposition (see further Brennies 1988).

The special type of opposed utterance that is the precursor to my informants' arguments is best described as consisting both of a *difference* in understanding the "antecedent event", and an *intention to influence* the other's behavior or attitude to the issue in question. An example of this is the following:

> He drinks too much. Most of our fights start with me getting impatient with his drinking. His daily rhythm is disrupted when he drinks. He can stay up and party all night, sleep all day, and then party again all night. That makes it impossible for me to relax. And he blows a lot of money this way. Our fights are often about money. His defense is often 'This has nothing to do with you. This is my life.' That type of answer saddens me every time. (Ruth H, individual interview)

Ruth's utterance reveals that she and her husband have divergent views of the issue at hand, and that she has communicated her view to her husband – and the message is that he should drink less. She offers several arguments for why her view ought to be seen as the correct one, and she briefly describes her husband's reaction.

In order to illustrate this form of reasoning, let me now give an ambiguous example of an opposed utterance:

I have never met such a suspicious person before. It's as if someone is always trying to hurt her. I was sitting the other day and feeding our kid... I asked her to hand me some paper towels... So she threw the dishrag right in my face, which really pissed me off! (Fredrik P, individual interview)

It is not entirely clear here if Fredrik is actually expressing an opposition in the sense of expressing a different attitude to his wife's behavior and an intention to influence her behavior. Fredrik claims instead to have communicated something entirely different ("I just asked her to hand me some paper towels"), a request that the wife interpreted as a criticism of her behavior for the purpose of changing this behavior, an interpretation which the husband refutes ("I have never met such a suspicious person"). The example has an opening statement, ambiguous as to whether it actually does contain an opposition in the sense indicated above and expressed in Ruth's utterance about her husband's drinking habits. Fredrik felt that his wife's reaction, on the other hand, indicates that she interpreted his utterance as an opposition.

The list of phrases which initiate arguments is a long one. According to my informants, any activity or behavior can potentially be opposed and can serve as the start of a verbal fight. This is in and of itself not unreasonable. On the contrary, to be dissatisfied or discontented with another human being is part of our everyday life. Our interaction with others continually places us in contradictory or paradoxical situations, which may lead to conflicts. The literature on family interaction focuses on how these conflicts between family members can be solved. According to the prevailing view in the literature, the problem-solving strategy is a distinctive feature of a family system. Families with an inadequate ability to transform disputes into settlements are considered dysfunctional (Cromwell and Olson 1975; Hoffman 1981; Matthews 1988).

As a result of what my informants told me, I became interested in the strategies the couples used for problem-solving. During our conversations, strong feelings of grief and powerlessness were revealed, but I uncovered little evidence of what could be called a problem-solving strategy:

I don't know what I am going to do. I just keep wondering why; it is as if I keep going around and waiting for him to change, or thinking that everything was going to be different. But it is wrong to wait for other people to change. Maybe I should change myself too, like getting angry and saying no, this is not the life I want to live. There has to be a change. When I get angry, it is usually at the wrong time, and usually leads to more fighting. Then afterwards, I am so sad that I cannot talk to him.

> I am more likely to walk around and wonder 'why does it have to be like this, why do I always have to be so sad?' . (Ruth H, individual interview)

According to the criteria outlined in the literature on family interaction, my informant couples could be classified as dysfunctional due to their lack of problem-solving strategies (Hoffman 1981). Furthermore, their narratives revealed an extremely local perspective. The opposed utterances were generally made abruptly in commonplace situations, and triggered a verbal aggressive episode that seemed to be lacking in context.

My preliminary data analysis consisted of attempts to classify the informant couples in terms of systemic dysfunctionality, due to the absence of problem-solving strategies. Attempting to understand the couples' verbal aggressive behavior, however, proved impossible. In fact, these attempts seriously challenge the idea of marital argumentative behavior as a problem-solving activity. As a consequence, my analytical perspective shifted to that of verbal marital aggression as a valid enterprise in its own right. The concept of "valid enterprise" here refers to the structure and procedures used by the couples to construct the verbal aggressive act. This way of approaching my data proved more successful, in the sense of making it possible to enhance my understanding of what had happened in the lead-up to the violent phase.

Here I have discussed the opening phase as if there were no possible disagreement as to when it all started. Every person who has ever argued with another person knows that this is not usually very easy to pinpoint. In actuality, it is precisely this issue that can lead to fights: "Who started this fight?" The arguments I describe are all similar on this point. In my male informants' narratives, the woman made the first move by unjustly accusing her husband – and vice versa in the women's accounts.

These different means of accounting for the start partly originate in the different positions held in the opening phase. "You started it", Ruth's husband may be motivated in claiming, being the object for discontent that he is. "You started it", Ruth may also be justified in claiming, as the person who lives with a husband who torments her with his drinking. Both parties seem justified in arguing that the other "is picking a fight", that is, forwarding argumentation as to what can be classified as the initial phase.

An opposed utterance related to the joint marital project

Generally speaking, once an opposition has been uttered in an interactional sequence it can be treated in a variety of ways. A full-blown argument or dispute has only one possible and contingent outcome, as determined by the next speaker (Sacks et al. 1974).

A prototype for how disagreements and differences in viewpoints need not necessarily lead to arguments, but rather to solutions to the problem could be summarized in four points:

(1) The first speaker makes an opening statement that indicates what the difference involves, while also indicating the way in which the difference represents a problem.

(2) The first and second speaker discuss the matter, together confirming or reformulating the issue.

(3) This discussion presupposes that a solution to the problem is being considered.

(4) The conclusion implies that the parties agree upon a solution and do in fact solve the situation.

The opening utterances described by my informants never followed the script written above as to what constitutes an opening to a discussion or argument. The second speaker disagreed with the opening utterance in a way which conferred relevance to the first speaker's utterance as a prelude to dispute, and not as a prelude to problem-solving. The interpretative frame used by the second speaker for reaching that conclusion was kept hidden from me, though, and even worse, was likewise hidden from both speakers. The first speaker most frequently referred to the second speaker's reaction as incomprehensible, and the second speaker referred to feelings of anger and the obvious impertinence displayed by the first speaker. To exemplify this, let us return to the sequence where a verbal fight is brewing between Fredrik and Nina P. Fredrik has asked for some paper towels, and Nina has thrown a dishrag in his face. Her comment about his actions is the following:

You should have heard his tone of voice: PAPER TOWELS! PAPER! It was horrible the way he shouted. He has really mastered the art of humiliating another person. He never shows me any respect. I have a lot of affection inside me – both that I want to give and that I want to get. But it's just not happening here. I am rather sensitive... It is easy for me to take things to heart. I feel like a failure and pretty worthless. (Nina P, joint interview)

Nina's reaction and comments were filled with feeling, and when she spoke her body language communicated how angry and hurt she had been and still was. During the interview, Fredrik made it clear that he absolutely did not understand what had happened in their kitchen on the evening in question. He said that he had needed her assistance at that moment and had had no ulterior motives. Feeding the child had simply turned into a rather messy affair. Her perception of the event was entirely different. She claimed that when Fredrik asked for paper, he was signaling discontent and resentment.

Urho H, husband to the earlier quoted Ruth H, makes the following comment about his reaction to her statements about his drinking habits:

> Until this happened, she'd been so great... I think it started when we bought this apartment... Suddenly, everything became so unreal...and hyped up. My old friends were no longer good enough... If I go and take a few beers or drinks... she hassles me so much about that... I don't think it's any of her business. A person ought to be allowed to relax sometimes... (Urho H, individual interview)

Considerable listening was needed before I understood that there was a "link missing" in my informants' narratives, a link that contained the interpretative framework used by the second speaker to interpret the first speaker's utterance as an invitation to a verbal fight. It was when I first discovered more about my informants' joint marital projects that I identified this link. Only then did their descriptions of what had happened in the argument's opening phase appear to be logical.

What happens in the argument's initial phase can be an expression by the first speaker of a difference in viewpoint from that of the second speaker who, in light of their joint marital project, interprets this utterance as unfair, provocative, and belligerent. In this way, the problem is never defined in relation to the specific issue that is the subject of the difference of opinion, such as the one party's alcohol habits, and that could have served as the subject of discussion and resolution.

It is also entirely possible that the couple has developed strategies for solving the problems, and that they might have been able to describe these had I asked them about an argument in which a problem was identified calling for a concrete solution. What they related was nothing like that. What they described was how the violent act began. In this context, no problems were solved.

Accordingly, a possible solution of differences and disagreements within a marriage through interaction characterized by the four points listed above for problem-solving, may presuppose a problem that consists of a concrete issue and not one where, as in this case, the parties' positions and relationships to each other as spouses come into question. The subheading of the analyzed disputes could be formulated as follows: "As my husband, you cannot act like this"; "As my wife, you cannot act like this". The precise content of such statements differs from couple to couple, depending on the design of their joint marital project. Nevertheless, the fundamental significance is similar for all couples.

The observation that the opening phase of an argument is closely related to the couple's marital project inspired me to reread what the informants had told me about these projects. What I was looking for were similarities and differences in the couples' means of organizing their joint projects that might shed light on the specific significance of a statement such as "As my husband, you cannot act like this".

In light of descriptions by feminist researchers of violent marriages (Dobash and Dobash 1979; Walker 1979; Christensen 1984; Lundgren 1985), I expected an over-representation of what was described in chapter 2 as "traditional marriages", where the relationship was based on the man's domination and a clear gender-bound division of labor. But my expectations were not born out by my material. The analysis of the couple projects indicated a broader span of modes of organizing married life.

At this point in the discussion, I would like to digress briefly in order to describe my informants' marital projects. However, my material on this point is such that any deductions must remain greatly uncertain. Therefore, the following should be viewed as a schematic presentation, which only with further material could be made more complete. Nevertheless, understanding what happens during all phases of a violent event requires a basic insight into the couples' marital projects.

The basic organization of the marital projects

For the purpose of gaining insight into the basic organization of the joint marital projects, I used the descriptions given by the informants and classified the marital projects on the basis of two principles that in part overlap one another. My first task was to determine whether the marital project was organized *primarily* according to the principle of complementarity or to the principle of symmetry. I found that the material contained two groups of nearly equal size, that is nine couples who organized their marital project along the complementary lines, and eleven that expressed the ambition to organize their marital life along symmetrical lines. My second task was to determine whether the parties were agreed or not about how the marital project was to be organized. A majority (12) of the couples were agreed, while the rest were not.

Of the nine couples who organized their couple project along complementary lines, five lived in traditional marriages with rigid role division. In three of these couples (Ulla and Hans A; Sonja and Per B; Angela and Pablo J), both parties claimed to be quite satisfied with the arrangement, while there was great discord in the other two cases as to the organization of the marital projects. In both cases, the men (Refa D and Ove T) wanted, and had succeeded, in keeping the women (Fathima D and Pirjo T) at home to care for the family. Their wives were openly discontented.

The remaining four "complementary" couples lived "traditionally" to the degree that the women had the responsibility for home and children. However, these women were not as oriented towards the home as were the women in the previously described marriages. These four women either worked outside the home or studied. Three of them (Pia I; Annika R; and Irene E) were satisfied with the arrangement. One of the women (Marie G) was extremely dissatisfied and believed that her husband's most cherished desire was to "chain her to the stove", something that she had avoided by acquiring her own source of income:

> He's still living in the forties and seems to think I am too. Women should stand at the stove and keep their mouths shut. When he's upset, he's allowed to scream and threaten. He's good at his job, so I can't complain about that. But he's prepared to go to any lengths to have a 1940s family. (Marie G, individual interview)

To sum up, six of the couples who organized their marital project along complementary lines agreed about this arrangement; three of the complementary organized couples disagreed about this way of organizing the marital life. What these three couples have in common is that the men established a life style which was primarily based on complementarity, but this was done over their wife's protests (table 4:1).

The remaining eleven of my informant couples expressed the ambition to organize their marital projects along symmetrical lines, and I categorized them on this basis. The ideal of the symmetrical marriage in terms of an "equal marriage" or a "marriage of comradery" was thus not attained by any of the couples, as far as I could understand. In accordance with Haavind's description of what is characteristic for the modern marriage, these marriages had "quasi-

egalitarian'' features (Haavind 1985). The women consistently held
the primary responsibility for the children, even if the men expressed
the wish to share this responsibility to a greater degree than did the
"traditional men". In contrast, the women shared the responsibility
of supporting the families with their husbands. Two of the women
(Lisa Q and Louise K) were highly educated with incomes higher
than their husbands'. Three of the women (Ruth H, Lena S, and
Kristina L) were essentially the breadwinners of their families, due to
their higher earning husbands' alcohol problems.

Six couples were agreed as to their desire to attain a symmetrical
living pattern. Three of them built their marital project around a
positive similarity of values, as expressed in the saying "two can do
better than one" (Ruth and Urho H; Maria and Victor F; Katrin and
Hector C).

One of these couples, the above quoted Ruth and Urho H, had lived in extreme poverty as children and had early on joined together
in a dream for a better life for themselves and their children. Their
life projects depended on the marital project for success. They were
prepared to work very hard to realize this dream for a home, security,
and a socially acceptable status.

The remaining three (Viveka and Adam N; Gunilla and Rolf M;
Susanne and Paul O) of the six couples who agreed on symmetrical
patterns built their marital projects on what could be described as a
negative similarity of values, as reflected in the expression "this is
the best I can do". Both the men and the women in these marriages
had several failed relationships behind them. They had been let down
and rejected. None of them displayed a strong emotional bond with
their partner, and they had entered into the marital project in hopes
of improving their own life projects. One of the women, Gunilla M,
related how she had had "bad luck in love" many times and had been
left. She met her current husband through a contact ad in the
newspaper. She could not recall what attracted her to him, "but he
had a job, which was more than most of the men who had answered
the ad".

Five of the couples who had organized their marital life according
to symmetrical principles disagreed about the arrangement. While
three of the women – and none of the men – living in some form of
complementarity expressed dissatisfaction with the arrangement, the
situation here was the opposite. In all five of the symmetrical marriages where dissatisfaction was expressed, it was the men who were
dissatisfied. One example of such a marriage is that of Lisa and
Ismeth Q.

Lisa comes from a Swedish middle-class environment in a small town in southern Sweden. Ismeth comes from a large lower-middle class family in a big city in Asia Minor. He came to Sweden as a child. His ambitions are high, and he appreciates Lisa's "class" and good education. They met at her workplace where he was on a temporary assignment as translator. They have built up their marriage on the principles of harmony and symmetry. Ismeth chose Lisa because he perceived her as somewhat his social superior, which suited his social ambitions well.

In the beginning, both were content with the situation. Lisa thought she had found the man of her dreams: considerate, warm, active in household work. But Ismeth grew increasingly discontented. As time passed, his picture of his wife changed. He started finding her dominating and unfeminine. He became more and more dissatisfied with their marital project:

> It probably was all wrong from the beginning. When I met Lisa, I was down and felt lonely. I was a little impressed by her; she was well educated. And she was very calm. But she's starting to irritate me more and more... and it's becoming clearer all the time that it's her who wants to hold the reins.... It's gotten worse and worse. She even tries to boss me around in front of my family, sitting there like a pasha and ordering me to 'do this and do that'. (Ismeth Q, individual interview)

Ismeth dreams about being back in his first marriage. His former wife had been a warm, feminine, and a "real" woman who devoted herself to him and their son, and who would never have even contemplated humiliating him the way Lisa does. He deeply regrets that divorce.

The description of Lisa and Ismeth's marriage leads us back to the question of what a "Swedish" marriage is. When categorizing the informants' marital projects, I was unable to find any systematic difference between a "totally Swedish" marriage and "other" marriages in terms of the organization of the marital project. On the other hand, each couple had its own history, of which the spouse's country of origin was a part. Lisa and Ismeth's marriage was an example of this. I shall give another.

Fathima and Refa D both worked as teachers in their original country. They were economically well-off and enjoyed a broad network of supportive relatives. They met as students at the university and organized their ensuing marriage along symmetrical lines. Refa's political activism is what drove him and his family into exile.

Refa anticipates the family's return to his home country after circumstances change there. He is working very hard in Sweden to establish a solid economy for this return. As there are no longer relatives able to assist with child and household care, this is a burdensome task. Thus, he believes that a "traditional marriage" where Fathima stays home is now in "everyone's best interest".

Fathima does not totally share his vision. She does not believe that the family is going to return to their home country. Should it become possible one day, she thinks that the children will be too "Swedish" to want to move there. Her view is that it is wisest to build up a life here in Sweden. She wants to recreate their former marital project where both worked making it possible to move into a better home.

The chasm between the spouses is deep on this point. Refa, who had never before raised a hand to his wife and who never believed he could do such a thing, attacks her physically in their Swedish exile which both believed would be peaceful. This seriously troubles him.

To sum up, six of the couples who organized their marital project along the symmetrical lines agreed about this arrangement. Five of the symmetrical organized couples disagreed about this way of organizing their marital life. What these couples have in common is that the women were successful in establishing a lifestyle primarily based on symmetry, but it was done over their husbands' protests (Table 4:1)

	Accordant	Discordant
Symmetry	6	5*
Complementarity	6	3**

* all opposed by the husbands
** all opposed by the wives

Table 4:1. Basic organization of the marital projects

Here I would like to end the digression from the main subject of this chapter and return to the study of the verbally aggressive act. I will give two examples of the initial phase of a verbal fight, the first one taken from an accordant, traditional marriage and the second one taken from a discordant, quasi-egalitarian marriage.

Prelude to arguments in an accordant, complementary (traditional) marriage

Ulla and Hans A live in a traditional marriage with which they both claim to be quite content. Hans sympathizes with all husbands of women who prefer to invest their energies outside the family and who may even lack the ability to create a beautiful home and a harmonious family life. For her part, Ulla sympathizes with all women who do not have bread-winning husbands who then have to leave their children in the hands of strangers so that they, the women, can go out and earn a living. In Ulla's and Hans' marriage, *Friday evenings* have a strong symbolic value. On that evening, their joint marital project is to be celebrated. Ulla's contribution is a well-prepared dinner in a pleasing atmosphere made economically feasible by Hans. Both are expected to appreciate this and to show their appreciation. Then, what is not supposed to happen, happens:

> He sat down in front of the TV and FELL ASLEEP. I think he almost started snoring... OK, he had had a few drinks. I can take quite a bit, but this builds up inside of me and then I just explode. Do you understand? It is difficult to explain, but whatever it is, I explode and he dismisses it with 'for that unimportant thing'. But it's not just that. It's this and that and this and that. He had hardly finished eating.... I mean all that we had agreed to do .... (Ulla A, joint interview)

Hans' comments were:

> Dammit, I can understand that she got pissed off.... I was too in a way, 'coz I didn't want to fall asleep... She doesn't think I appreciate her, which I can understand after everything that's happened... But what I appreciate the most is that she makes such a nice home for us. And she's really a good mother. She takes care of us. Warm... But I also do everything for the family, in the way I am able to. Sometimes I get tired, but that's because I work so much. There's no 40 hours a week, more like 60. Plus all the night work with bookkeeping and the like. I think she could understand.... (Hans A, joint interview)

Both Ulla and Hans are willing to restrict their individual freedom in order to attain something else together, in their highly valued marriage. Ulla makes their lives pleasant, and Hans works hard. This gives them a reciprocal right to demand things in the name of the joint marital project. Conflicts arise when one of them demands something he or she thinks is legitimate in light of the marital project, but which is refuted by the other. Hans does not think that he has discredited Ulla or their marriage when he falls asleep in front of the television, because he was simply overly tired. Ulla is of the opposite view.

Prelude to arguments in a discordant, symmetrical (quasi-egalitarian) marriage

To be part of a marital project where there is disagreement about its fundamental orientation means that in addition to a latent conflict between the life projects and the marital project, there is also a constant uncertainty as to the continued existence of the marital project. How can there be a unity when there is discord about the most basic aspects? Living in such a marital project must mean that thoughts of escape and separation become part of the marital project as well as pondering about whether one's spouse cares and intends to stay. Thus, the *theme of trust* and the *theme of caring* are continually exposed in a painful way.

After these introductory remarks, I would like to quote Nina P's description of her and Fredrik's marriage:

> I have goals for this life. I have wanted to better myself and attain a certain status. Fredrik wants exactly the same thing. He has class. He has ambition. He knows, just like I do, what he wants out of life, and you don't get there on your own. (Nina P, individual interview)

When Fredrik met Nina, he thought that she was the perfect life companion, cheerful and optimistic and with the same attitude to life as he had. They got married and had a daughter. With time, both Nina and Fredrik started doubting whether they had really found the right person in the other:

> We have had a good marriage, but there's no doubt that it has gotten worse and worse as time goes on... To describe our sex life as a refrigerator would be misleading, like a freezer would be more accurate... And Nina has some drinking problems. She can't handle alcohol like normal people and *pours down* everything she can get her hands on and gets drunk and provocative and acts totally undignified. (Fredrik P, individual interview)

Fredrik's life project is more important for him than the joint marital project in that he married Nina after deciding that his chances for attaining his goals were better within the framework of a joint marital project. As he starts doubting whether Nina can really fulfill her side of the bargain in the marital project, thus jeopardizing his life project, his view of the marital project is becoming increasingly negative. Nina views the ability to give and receive emotional support as an important aspect of her life project and has become less supportive of Fredrik's efforts to convert their marital project into an endeavor for material success:

> I have a lot of affection inside me – both that I want to give and that I want to get. But it's just not happening here... He's too conceited. I don't know what he's thinking these days. He wants more and more things. And when we argue, the only thing that means anything to him is the house. (Nina P, individual interview)

To live in a marriage of discord does not primarily mean struggling over the basic choices of how the joint marital life is designed in a formal, principal meaning. Instead it means living in a marriage, the existence of which is in constant doubt, and where the basic human needs of trust and caring are consistently neglected.

The reaction phase: The verbal abusive attacks

To summarize, my informants characterized the initial phase of their verbal fights with the following exchange:

> First turn: An utterance, which is constructed as an opposition about a commonplace issue.

> Second turn: A disapproval of this utterance, expressed in a way that confers relevance to the first utterance as a prelude to dispute.

According to the logical order of this exchange, I expected a reaction to the second turn in the form of a continuation of the first speaker's disapproval of the second speaker's utterances. No such reaction was found in my informants' narratives. What was found, however, was the frequent use of a turn, not meant as an opposition to prior *utterances,* but more as an opposition to the general competence and *personal characteristics* or *status* of the person making the utterance in question.

The reaction that followed the two turns which initiated the verbal fight seemed to be composed essentially of pejorative personal descriptions and insults. The person portrayed and constituted through these utterances was a clearly restricted person with a status that was being questioned:

> When things are calm, we are able to say 'we have to talk, the two of us, we can't keep holding it in'. But then nothing happens. When we start arguing, I say exactly what I think and feel. Everything that I had been carrying around wanting to say comes out then. Not very flattering things. And he can't deal with this, with me throwing these things in his face. He goes completely crazy. (Nina P, joint interview)

In contrast to the common idea that female interaction is characterized by politeness and an aversion to fighting, I found my female informants equally competent in this kind of activity as were the men:

> Even when I'm very angry, I can go around, cold, saying nothing. Or I can keep on fussing about something without really showing that I am upset about it. It drives him crazy that I don't give up. I can restrain myself, and I know how to handle him. I know how to hurt him. I say those mean things that I know are going to really get to him. The content of what I say varies from occasion to occasion, depending on what he is sensitive about just then. (Irene E, individual interview)

According to what both the men and the women said, the types of arguments used by the women seemed to be more advanced and complex than those of the men. The women seemed to know more about their men than vice versa. Knowledge about the other party, especially about weaknesses and sensitivities, was considered to be valuable in this kind of verbal fighting. The above quoted Irene E. described the kind of knowledge she used as she counterattacked her husband during their fights:

> His image is tough, but I know that inside he is rather insecure. He had a pretty bad childhood. He doesn't like to open up. It took a long time before he... could express what he thought. He has a complex about everything. He never shows his weak sides, and he is the type who believes that you never let anyone else get involved in your problems. Other people just want to use and hurt you. He believes that. People look for scandals and love it when someone else feels bad. (Irene E, individual interview)

Vladimir E, the husband of Irene E repeatedly described his wife as nice but a nag who never listened to him:

> When she starts harping about something, and doesn't stop, I get real down. Then we have an argument. That's when I start reacting like a human being. She's always nagging about my drinking, even if a whole week goes by without a drop, or even 14 days, she just keeps nagging.... (Vladimir E, joint interview)

The description of the nagging woman, who does not listen, who is impossible to reach with words, who attacks with violent verbal attacks, was a recurring theme in my informants' narratives. The following quotation comes from the already frequently quoted Fredrik P:

She has all her claws out and it's impossible to penetrate her armor or shield or whatever you want to call it. Everything I say to her gets thrown back in my face. You'd think that the laws of probability would mean I'd be right at least once in two years. But never once have I been right in what I've said to her. It is impossible to talk to her, and she never listens to what I have to say. I always get it back – twice as bad. (Fredrik P, joint interview)

The communication of worthlessness

Characteristic of the utterances during the reaction phase was their suggestion of the speaker as "the one up" who was trying to "put down" the other. In other words, the main feature of the reaction phase can essentially be described as the *communication of worthlessness.*

The narratives contain many examples of how this was achieved. I have classified the utterances which are well adapted for the communication of worthlessness by *content* as,

– the use of weaknesses,
– the use of embarrassing events, or
– the use of bad traits of the other party.

Furthermore, I have classified them according to the *quality of the words used,* such as,

– the use of a definite utterance,

and by the *quantity* of words, where

– silence as well as
– a voluminous amount of words could be used.

The use of weakness
"He has a complex about everything", one of my female informants tells me. She continues, "I know how to handle him, and I say mean things that I know will *get to him.* He believes everything I say. If I say, 'God, you look terrible; I can't stand to be with you' he can run around an entire day worrying about his appearance" (Irene E, individual interview).

The kind of weakness exploited could, as in this example, be related to the perceived physical or spiritual weakness of the other person. It can also touch upon the most central and sensitive aspects of the marital project, such as closeness and trust:

> I have a lot of affection... both that I want to give and that I want to get. But it's just not happening here.... I am rather sensitive.... I get upset rather easily .... It's as if I don't mean anything to him, like that he could leave me any time if he weren't so crazy about our house. Then I get sad, and feel like a failure, like I'm worthless. (Nina P, joint interview)

The use of embarrassing events
The most useful events for communicating worthlessness to one's partner are events during which the latter behaved in a way disdained even by that person. One of my female informants gave me an example of this. Nina P's narrative reveals how this can be used.

When Nina and Fredrik met, both had good jobs, and lived stable lives. After they had known each other for a while, she confided in him that her previous life had been anything but settled. Her childhood home was a mess, and she more or less got kicked out when she was a teenager. She escaped at one point and lived a vagrant's life which included some drug abuse. Eventually, her parents helped her rent an apartment after she had reached rock bottom from drugs and despair. Finally, she sought psychiatric help, which was the turning point in her life.

Nina told Fredrik about all this while they were still very infatuated with each other, and he had been empathetic. She felt that her painful story had brought them closer to one another. Fredrik was later to exploit her confidences during their arguments:

> He claims he dragged me out of the slums. That's not true and it is disgusting of him to say such a thing. I can't deny it, because there's some truth in it. Like using the fact that I told him I had used drugs over a five-month period. He takes advantage of what I said to him in the strictest confidence when he says that I have an alcohol problem now. I think that this is a violation of my confidence. But he uses things like that. (Nina P, joint interview)

During the verbal fight, Nina's life-history was rewritten by Fredrik. He betrayed her reliance. He was entrusted with the task of confidence that he abused when he used her past as proof of her wickedness. His attacks had a tremendous impact on her self-confidence. Strong feelings of guilt and self-hatred were linked with her youth. She was ashamed about her previous life, and ashamed at being exposed. She was ashamed at being a victim of her own desire to come close to someone. She derided herself for being so stupid as to have thought that she could ever be worthy of someone's love and respect.

The use of bad traits

A sensitive event can be replaced by a sensitive trait that is ascribed to one's partner. If the partner views this trait negatively, but perceives him- or herself as carrier of it, the possibility exists to communicate worthlessness by charging that person with that bad trait.

Ulla relates that Hans often calls her "whore" during their arguments. She says this makes her mad, but does not really shake her up, because she knows it's not true:

> There's just some things there's no point in saying, because they have no effect. But the opposite is true for other things. They can break you completely. (Ulla A, joint interview)

What Ulla could get most upset about was when Hans indicated that he doubted her intellectual capacity. His standard expression was: "As dumb in the head as you are, one would think you would be in a special class". In her turn, she pointed out that "there are so many good-looking guys around" and "lots of them are standing in line for me". Her most effective comment was "I don't talk to under-aged boys". Her comments encroached on her husband's male ego. He was ten years her junior. He was not pleased with his own appearance, and he felt fat, inexperienced, and immature.

The majority of couples had several terms for each other's more sensitive traits. These concepts first attained their full force within the marital project and within the specific argument. An expression such as "I don't talk to under-aged boys" would be almost comical in another context. Classic put-downs such as "fatso", "you disgusting fat pig", or "you toad", refer to bodily deficiencies and identify the other person as unattractive and repulsive. Concepts such as "bum", "pimple-face", "slob", touch upon the object's social status. These types of comments have some potential effect within the framework of many marital projects. But the man who wants to communicate worthlessness to his wife by calling her "you disgusting fat pig" is helped if his wife does not happen to be slim as a model.

The use of "definite" talk

A recurring theme in the descriptions of the argument was that it led to confusion since the other person "did not tell the truth". The spouse's belief that it was possible amidst the tangle of accusations

and counter-accusations to establish the truth and lies was so strong
that the parties became confused when they did not succeed in doing
so.

A contributory cause for their confusion was their use of language
in a way that could be designated *"definite" talk.* Described using
"definite" talk, things happen *never* or *always,* when they most probably happen *seldom* or *often.* "Definite" talk omits everything
specific, and touches upon every subject with a general sweep.

The use of silence and the voluminous use of words

Even if the arguments are described primarily as verbal activities
with a high noise level, *silence* is used as a means of communicating
worthlessness. One of the women describes an argument that lasted
the several days that her husband refused to talk to her:

> Right in the middle of our argument, he left and went to a friend's house
> and came home late. I was very upset when he came back, but he only
> said he was 'very sorry'. He had nothing more to say about it, and then
> said nothing for days... I felt... I was just empty. I couldn't eat for many
> days. I felt so bloody bad you wouldn't believe it. If you want to totally
> destroy someone, that is the way to do it. I don't understand what kind
> of person could do such a thing. (Gunilla M, individual interview)

Thus, it is not only the quality of language that is an instrument in
an argument, but also its quantity. Silence can be used, but so can
voluminous talking. A common Swedish saying can be translated as
"talking until the other person falls over". This saying depicts a person who by means not of skillful argumentation but rather of the
volume of words steamrolls his or her counterpart.

A first note on social order

The overall purpose of my analysis so far has been to describe the
basic structure of the marital verbal fight as it serves as the pre-
history to woman battering in my informants' narrative accounts. I
have used time as an organizing factor for the text, and related the
structural aspects to the time factor, while describing the initial
phase and the reaction phase of the verbal fight.

As the spouses fight verbally, they also create basic forms of social
organization. My description of the structure of the verbal aggressive
act in part concerns the marital organization. To finish the description of the verbal aggressive act, I will make some remarks about the

kinds of social order in the marriage that could be the outcome of this kind of interaction.

Characteristic of the utterances made during the reaction phase were depictions of the speaker as "the one up" who was attempting to "put down" the other. I used the expression "to communicate worthlessness" to describe this quality. Consequently, a prominent feature of the social process underway during the verbal fight could be described as an endeavor to question the status of the other person, and to demote him or her to a lower ranking. The social order produced by this activity could be suitably described as a hierarchical organization of the marital project. In this process, the verbal fight played a constitutive role.

My description of utterances which are well adapted for communicating worthlessness showed how a *hierarchical social order* of my informants' marital projects was formulated, refuted, and reconstituted by means of the turn taking during the reaction phase. In this respect, I did not find any difference between those couples whose basic organizational principle was complementarity, as in the traditional marriages, and those who sought symmetry in a quasi-egalitarian format. According to my informants' narratives, participating in an argument that results in a hierarchical social order where the parties are in a struggle to gain an advantage over their partners may apparently occur just as easily in a traditional marriage as in a quasi-egalitarian one, where responsibility is shared for the support of the family.

Neither a pattern of coexistence, nor a hierarchically conducted social order, however, are fixed categories, but rather are relations which are reproduced by the regularity of particular actions. As the spouses interact in the opening phase of the violent incident, they create a fundamental form of social order. I will return to the question of how this kind of social order evolves over time.

The termination of the verbal aggressive act

With few exceptions, my informants' narratives all contained evidence of exceptional difficulty in ending the verbal fight. The spouses seemed bound to the fight by numerous factors: The rhetoric itself bound them, since the recurring sequence of opposition-reaction contained no terminating phase. The notion of marital fighting as a problem-solving activity bound them, as they continued in their hope that the argument would end in resolution. The next chapter is devoted to the violent incident. Except for this means of terminating the verbal fight, two others were mentioned:

– interruption by children, neighbors, or friends, for example, a child demanding attention or a neighbor complaining about the noise.
– the resignation of the woman, that is, if the woman indicates submission, the argument can come to a stop. The majority of female informants knew how to do this, but were also aware of what it did to their life project:

Sometimes, when I've been really afraid, I've walked around like in a vacuum. When the fear gets to be too much... then I disappear... I get apathetic.. I stare, get paralyzed. But then all unpleasantness disappears... Everything seems meaningless. He usually stops then... but sometimes keeps going on and on... He gets angry if he doesn't get a response... (Ruth H, individual interview)

You know, I have sometimes been able to calm him down./.../ That would mean that I was giving in to him and that would be the same as admitting that I had been wrong. /.../ I have tried many times to say 'let's stop talking now; each of us can have an opinion', but he refuses. He insists on telling me how wrong I really am... (Irene E, individual interview)

When I review my informants' accounts in order to discover what they said about stopping their arguments, it was not only what they said that captured my attention, but also what they *did not say*. I can list at least five possible ways to end an argument that do not seem to have occurred to, or been used by, my informants:

– *he leaves*
– *she leaves*
– *he adopts the subordinate position*
– *they switch the form of interaction and identify a problem that is possible to solve*
– *they admit that they are hurting one another and, by defining the situation as such, can stop arguing.*

My amazement at what was *missing* from the accounts was consistently greater than my amazement at what I *did find* in them. The couples' repertory of behavior patterns in conflict situations was strikingly limited. My cautious conclusion is that a common trait of my informants' marital projects is a rigid power structure of dominant/subordinate positions, as well as a tendency to refrain from taking responsibility for one's own behavior during an argument and to blame the other party. To argue that "*I am* doing this because my partner is doing that" is much more common in my informants' accounts than an argument such as "*I am* doing this because my feelings have been hurt".

When no verbal aggressive act precedes the violent act
The two exceptions:

1. The desire for revenge as pre-history of the violent act
Two of my informants' accounts of the pre-history to the violent incident differ from the other eighteen. These people linked no verbal aggression to the violent outburst. In the first of these accounts, the wife, Lisa Q, describes the prelude to her marriage in the following way:

> When we first met, it was True Love from the start, for both of us. We quickly moved in together, after only a few months. I thought he was really affectionate, an emotional person, considerate, sensitive. All the good characteristics. Sometimes I was a little astounded at his temper. But I wasn't the target of it – I only saw it in other situations. (Lisa Q, individual interview)

In retrospect, her husband, Ismeth Q, did not view their first meeting and time together as positive. He referred to the relationship as something "most probably wrong from the start". As mentioned earlier, his view was that the marriage had taken unfortunate turns:

> I never thought she was particularly sexy. Later, that became a problem. I got more and more irritated when she dressed poorly and unwomanly. On top of that, she started deciding more and more, and after a while, she was in full command over me. 'Do this, do that'. No one can tell me what to do like that. We argued; she pushed my sensitive buttons the whole time, until we finally moved apart. (Ismeth Q, individual interview)

Lisa's account is consistently more upbeat. She describes two young people who plan a life together, who buy a row house, and who have children together. The conflicts that arose were not more than she thought possible to handle. There were fights about money and especially about her husband's work situation:

> He decided he wanted to go into business for himself. He started borrowing money to invest it. That turned into a conflict. I have no faith in his ability to manage his own business. You have to know a lot, but he thought he would be able to get it off the ground with no trouble. (Lisa Q, individual interview)

The conflict deepened between Lisa and Ismeth. Ismeth spent less and less time with his family, moved away from them, but returned. Finally, they decided to separate:

The way it was, you can understand why we got a divorce. But that wasn't the end of it. She still insisted on deciding everything. I couldn't even decide how to spend time with my child. I couldn't take her home. I had to sit and play with her in the sandbox. It was so humiliating, that feeling of someone else dictating the terms of my life. It was like she was sticking needles in me the whole time, and when I asked her why she did that, she denied it. It was horrid. Finally, I got obsessed with the idea of redressing these wrongs. There had to be justice. She had to be humiliated as much as I had been if I ever was to be free again. /.../ A film gave me the idea. A man who had been terrorized by his wife like I have, forced her outside naked and shamed her. So I went home to Lisa and my hate blinded me. I can't describe what happened. I brought a big knife along with me to force her to take off her clothes. (Ismeth Q, individual interview)

Ismeth did not wholly succeed in getting his wife to run outside naked in front of the neighbors, but the situation ended in aggravated assault. This violent incident will be further described in a following chapter.

2. Divorce as pre-history of the violent act

One of my informant couples accounted for their pre-history in terms of a painful divorce, unacceptable in the eyes of the man. This kind of account was most frequent in the police reports. A clear example of this kind of account is the following, taken from a police report. A woman summons the police to her apartment late one night. When the police arrive, they find a woman with a swollen face and kick marks on her legs. She told the following, as reported in the police report:

At about 9pm last night, my ex-husband showed up here. I told him I didn't want to see him, but he said he wanted to see the children. They had just gone to bed so I asked him to leave and closed the door. He didn't leave and kept begging to come in. After a while, it got quiet but then I heard him walking up and down the stairs. He started swearing and screaming and kicking the wall. The neighbors came out. They were furious and asked him what the hell was going on. He calmed down but didn't leave. Suddenly, he rang the bell again and begged and pleaded to come in. So I let him in. That was stupid, really stupid. But I was so sick of everything and embarrassed in front of the neighbors. I thought I could keep him calm. He first came in quietly and sat on the sofa in the living room. I asked him what he wanted, and told him that he couldn't just come around like this. Then he got angry and said that I always had to be so unpleasant. Then he got up and started circling around yelling that I probably had another man there. He talked about a lot of intimate things we had done. Then I noticed that he wasn't sober. I tried to get him out of there, and it was then he started hitting me. (Woman 36, summary, police report)

The man gave his version in the police record:

> I can't understand why she had to bring in the police. This is no police business, it is a family matter. We had a fight the other night. I was really sorry about it, but she really should take part of the blame. She can get really aggressive. We sat and talked and then she just decided to kick me out. She claims she has the right to, since we are divorced. Yeah, sure we are, but it depends on how you look at it. I mean, this is my family. She didn't like it when I drank. Constantly nagging. So I don't live with her anymore. But I don't dislike her and I love the kids. (Man, 41, my summary, police report)

This is a special type of discord, and the discord affects the definition of the relationship, a discord that could be described in terms of a *misunderstanding in the categorization of the relationship* – they are legally separated, but the legal separation has not been followed by any psychological separation on the husband's part.

The pre-history of the violent incident – a summary

The pre-histories to the violent incidents can be described, with two exceptions, as *unfinished argument sequences*. These argument sequences are characterized by a verbal interplay of the conflict type, where the focus of the interaction is shifted from the verbal *factual content* of the argument to the quarreling parties' *social status and personality traits*. This takes the form of comments by the quarreling parties about something that is part of the *joint marital* project and the *individual life projects*.

The *central issues* of the narratives of the pre-history can be concluded as follows:

– A (woman or man) *makes a request* of B (woman or man) to change action (e.g. stop talking, frame talk differently).

This request reflects a certain understanding of rights (on behalf of A) and *obligations* (on behalf of B) operating in the marital context of the couple in question.

– The request is refused by B, the refusal reflects a *denial* of rights (on behalf of A) and obligations (on behalf of B).

These two verbally exercised steps are repeated in a symmetrically escalating way: request follows refusal, follows request, follows refusal and so on.

The *content* of speech in these two verbally exercised steps can be said to be the *communication of the other person's "worthlessness"*. Verbal interactional strategies are adopted by the parties for the purpose of communicating worthlessness by evoking topics that are *sensitive* to the other person, such as embarrassing events, sensitive traits, weaknesses. The *quality* of the words may also make it possible to communicate worthlessness by the use of "definite" talk, and the same applies to the *quantity* of the words. Total silence or a torrent of words can both serve a purpose in this context.

This type of interaction creates a *social order* in the marriage which is characterized by a rigid hierarchical organization which contains a dominant and subordinate position, as well as the shifting of responsibility for one person's actions to his or her counterpart.

5

The Violent Incident in Figures

Introduction

In this chapter, an overview is given of the violent incident as found in the 141 cases of repeated violence taken from the police records and social welfare office files. The material is based on a review of available records as well as on information conveyed orally in those cases where the records were found to be insufficient. The following sources were used:

Police investigation records
Crime reports
Social welfare office files
Conversations with social workers

Forms of violence

When categorizing the violent events, the police look at whether the event can be considered as illegitimate or not. Police efforts are expected to result in a determination of whether a criminal act has been committed, if so, how the crime should be captioned, and against whom there are reasonable grounds for suspecting the criminal actions. In this process, establishing the kind of violence that had been used is essential. This determination is primarily based on information obtained during interrogations with the men.

The social worker investigates the individual's social situation in general, and not the violent incident in particular. In the 29 of the 141 cases which were known only to the social authorities, I was compelled in most cases to complement my information through conversations with the social worker. Despite these efforts, some information is still lacking about these 29 cases.

In the description of violence in the 141 cases, a *punch* is the most common type of act. In 124 cases, the man strikes the woman, and in 90 of these cases, the blow is serious (that is, he uses his fists). In 34 cases, he does not strike as hard as this, but instead strikes or slaps her with an open hand or shoves her, or pulls the woman's hair. In 49 cases, he *kicks* her. Twenty-one men *threatened the woman with some form of weapon,* possibly a chair, an extension cord for the vacuum cleaner, or a bottle. Fourteen men went further and used their weapons. (Table 5:1)

	No. of cases	Prop. (%)
Threats		
Not present	50	36
Minor	35	25
Serious	47	33
Information lacking	9	6
Total	141	100
Punches		
Not present	13	9
Open hand	26	18
With fist	90	64
Shoves	8	6
Information lacking	4	3
Total	141	100
Kicks		
Not present	84	60
Present	38	26
Serious	11	8
Information lacking	8	6
Total	141	100
Weapon		
Not present	88	63
Threatened to use it	21	15
Used it	14	10
Attempted choking	9	6
Information lacking	9	6
Total	141	100

Table 5:1 Forms of violence used by the men

The various categories of violence are not mutually exclusive. On the contrary, the most common pattern is for the men *to use several different forms of violence and for serious violence to subsume milder forms.*

What do the 141 cases say about the *frequency of this violence?* The general tendency is for several non-reported violent incidents to underlie each reported incident. (Table 5:2)

	No.of cases	Prop. (%)
No previous incident	2	1
At least once	22	16
More than one incident	55	39
Occurs		
Often	39	27
Regularly	19	14
Information lacking	4	3
Total	**141**	**100**

Table 5:2. Frequency of violence

Women's injuries

What can we see from the 141 cases about the women's *injuries?* Facial injuries are reported for 103 women. There is reason to assume that in cases where no mention is made of facial injury, there was in fact no such injury. Such obvious and serious injuries would surely be noted. The most common facial injury is bruises, that is, black-and-blue marks and swellings on the face, without fractures.

Bodily injuries were noted for 86 women; for 40 women, it was noted that there was no such injury, and information was lacking in 15 cases. These figures are not as reliable as those for facial injuries. They are primarily based on the women's accounts, and not on physical examinations by physicians. With regard to serious injuries – fractures and others – it ought to be assumed that the figures are correct since such injuries generally require hospitalization.

Sixty women exhibited or claimed to have symptoms of anxiety and worry. Six women said they were depressed, or appeared depressed to the police. Two women tried to commit suicide. (Table 5:3)

	No. of cases	Prop. (%)
Facial injuries		
None	23	16
Medium/minor	36	25
Black and blue	48	34
Fractures and other serious injuries	19	14
Information lacking	15	11
Total	**141**	**100**
Bodily injuries		
None	40	28
Medium/minor	41	29
Black and blue	31	22
Fractures and other serious injuries	14	10
Information lacking	15	11
Total	**141**	**100**
Mental injuries		
Not present	27	19
Anxiety	60	43
Depression	6	4
Attempted suicide	2	1
Information lacking	46	33
Total	**141**	**100**

Table 5:3 Battered women's injuries.

The general picture of marital violence in the 141 cases can be summarized as follows: A man hits his wife in the face with his fist, hard enough to bruise her face and cause black-and-blue marks and swelling. The violent action described in the police report is only one in a series of several such incidents.

Alcohol and marital woman battering

A substantial body of literature deals with the question of alcohol and violent interpersonal crimes. In their comprehensive review of the literature on alcohol and intrafamily violence, Kaufman Kantor and Straus summarize the findings from 15 empirical studies and include their own (Kaufman Kantor and Straus 1990). Kaufman Kantor and Straus contend that there is no consensus in the literature on even the elementary question of whether there is a correlation between drinking and intrafamily violence. The studies reviewed encompass a range of estimates of alcohol's presence in spousal violence from 6% to 85%. However, Kaufman Kantor and Straus found many methodological problems in these studies. Most used descriptive or bivariate statistics, and therefore lacked controls for confounding variables; some were based on clinical samples and others on more or less representative community samples, where a variety of measures for both alcohol and wife abuse were employed (Kaufman Kantor and Straus 1990 pp. 219–223).

In their own study, Kaufman Kantor and Straus performed a multivariate analysis in order to study three essential factors related to intrafamily violence: alcohol, social class, and norms about the use of violence. Using survey data based on a nationally representative sample of 5,159 couples, they examined three questions: (1) Do men who drink heavily have a higher probability of wife beating than those who do not? (2) To what extent does drinking occur at the time of the violent incident? (3) Are such linkages between drinking and wife beating found primarily among working-class men? Their findings revealed a strong link between alcohol use and physical abuse of wives. Alcohol was involved in about one out of four instances of wife abuse. Further, they found that the combination of blue-collar occupational status, drinking, and the approval of violence is associated with the highest likelihood of wife abuse. Men with these characteristics have a rate of wife abuse which is 7.8 times greater than the wife-abuse rate among white-collar men who drink little and who do not approve of slapping one's wife under any circumstances (Kaufman Kantor and Straus 1990 pp. 203–224).

In my own investigation of the link between wife battering and alcohol, the police reports revealed that 69 (49%) of the men and 46 (33%) of the women were under the influence of alcohol at the time of the violent incident. In 29 (20%) of the couples, both parties had been drinking. (Table 5:4)

I consider it difficult to draw any far-reaching conclusions about the degree to which alcohol is present during incidents of wife abuse based on my sample of police reports. It may be reasonable to assume that the police are more likely to intervene if one or both parties are drunk. On the other hand, battered women have commented on their intoxicated spouses' ability to appear sober when the police arrive (Reed et al. 1983). Finally, women may need to attribute the batterer's violence to alcohol as a means of comprehending the irrational and of excusing the violent event (Dobash and Dobash 1979; Gelles 1974).

Influence of alcohol among men	Influence of alcohol among the woman				
	Information lacking	No	Minor	Serious	Total
Information lacking	9	2	1	0	12
No	1	49	1	1	52
Minor	2	11	12	1	26
Serious	3	18	13	17	51
Total	**15**	**80**	**27**	**19**	**141**

Table 5:4 Influence of alcohol at the time of the violent incident.

In order to understand the impact of alcohol on the violent incident, I tested the correlation between the presence of alcohol and a series of variables such as reason for conflict, type of violence, injury, age, and so on. I found a correlation between the woman's serious injuries and the man or the woman being under the influence of alcohol. I here define the concept of "serious injury" as black and blue marks, fractures, or other serious injuries. 51 of the men were extremely intoxicated, and they caused 30 of the 67 cases of serious facial injuries, that is, 58% of these men caused serious injuries to their wives' faces, compared to 37% of the men who were not under the influence of alcohol. (Table 5:5)

Nineteen of the women were extremely intoxicated, and they were the victims of 13 of the serious facial injuries, that is, 68% of the extremely intoxicated women had serious facial injuries, compared to 36% of the women not under the influence of alcohol. (Table 5:6)

It may be reasonable to interpret these figures as indicating that the presence of alcohol makes it more difficult for both the man and the woman to control the situation. She has more difficulty in protecting herself, and he has more difficulty in keeping the assault within certain boundaries.

	Proportion (%) of cases of serious injury to women within each group of men's alcohol intoxication (absolute numbers given in parenthesis)	
	Facial (67)	Bodily (45)
Degree of man's alcohol intoxication (N=141)		
Information lacking (N=12)	25 (3)	17 (2)
No alcohol (N=52)	37 (19)	36 (18)
Lightly (N=26)	55 (15)	35 (9)
Extremely (N=51)	58 (30)	32 (16)

Table 5:5 Number of women's serious injuries and men's degree of alcohol intoxication.

	Proportion (%) of cases of serious injury to women within each group of their alcohol intoxication (absolute numbers given in parenthesis)	
	Facial (67)	Bodily (45)
Degree of woman's alcohol intoxication (N=141)		
Information lacking (N=15)	47 (7)	20 (3)
No alcohol (N=80)	36 (29)	36 (29)
Lightly (N=27)	67 (18)	26 (7)
Extremely (N=19)	68 (13)	32 (6)

Table 5:6 Number of women's serious injuries and their degree of alcohol intoxication

The violent incident in figures – a summary

In this chapter, a brief overview was given of the violent incident as found in the 141 cases of repeated violence taken from police records and social welfare office files. The violence mainly ranged from serious to medium-serious, where 49% of the men and 33% of the women were under the influence of alcohol. The woman's injuries proved to be more serious if she and/or the man were intoxicated at the time of the battering.

6

Accounts of the Violent Incident

Introduction

> It was just 'stop it, stop talking shit'. Like, I just didn't want to hear any more. I had heard enough. But I never wanted to hurt her. She means too much to me for that. The hitting is just a warning. Otherwise, I could just as well take a pistol and shoot her. I know I am hard-handed. She says so too. But I'm not hard on purpose. I am also soft. She admits that. But women are different from men. Women are psychologically stronger, they say. I just react: 'Now, dammit. You are going to keep quiet. Don't say another fucking word.' I don't say 'now you are going to get it so you die'. It is not like that. (Vladimir E, individual interview)

The fourth chapter revealed a remarkable concordance between the men's and women's narratives about the pre-history. Their narratives described pre-histories which had a narrow and consistent structure consisting of an inseparable sequence of events, each one following the other in chronological order. The accounts of the violent incidents allow no such concordance. After a first reading of the men's accounts, and a comparison with those of the women, it became clear that the accounts diverged substantially. Although the men and women took part in the same violent events, the men's stories generally revolved around a description of an incident they called "a fight" (Sw. "bråk"), while the women referred to what had happened as "an assault" (Sw. "misshandel"). Apparently, they made different sense of the same marital violent act.

After a subsequent reading of the accounts, this first impression of divergence faded to some degree. Once I started to identify the different languages being used, the descriptions became more concordant. Some aspects of the violent incident recurred in all narratives, seemingly an integral part of these incidents. The basic descriptions contained words locating the *scene* (the situation in which the violence occurred), indicating the *agents* that performed the acts (the man and the woman), suggesting the *purpose* of the violent act (why the man did what he did), and describing *how* he did it.

According to this basic form, the accounts then varied depending on whether the narrator was a man or a woman. The point of departure of the men's accounts was the purpose of the action, whereas the women mainly described what happened when the men assaulted them, and the consequences of these actions for them.

The quotation that opened this chapter was from Vladimir E. It was typical in its form and content of the men's manner of narrating. Pablo J's description of what happened when he hit his wife is a more uncommon form of narration:

> I think I hit her mainly with my hands... at first, at least, and then I pro-bably also kicked her. I hit her in the face, in the head, for I don't know how long. You can't tell how long it goes on. I mean, you're not thinking – you sort of go crazy/.../ I'm not sure where I kicked her. It could have been on her legs, but also her arms/.../ I feel so bloody bad about this now. I would like to have my wife here and say to her: 'Whatever happens, Angela, I love you! Do you understand, I love you, Angela' [starts to cry]/.../ She was swollen around the eyes, with a big bump over her eyebrow. (Pablo J, individual interview)

To understand the principles for structuring an account of the violent incident, we will have to return to the previous discussion on the marital violent act as a questionable marital action. A marital act considered as questionable challenges the stability and the continuity of the marital world. In other words, it challenges the joint marital project as well as the individual life projects. As we listen to the infor-mants' accounts of the violent incident, we are given a description of what it is that characterizes this incident. If we look not only at the content of these accounts, but also at their construction, the ac-counts enable us to understand how the informants deal with the conflict between their individual life projects and the marital project, on the one hand, and the questionable marital action, on the other.

Usually, we deal with challenging events in our lives by talking about them. In an attempt to render the events meaningful, we reflect on what happened, assign motives, and try to characterize the situation in the context of a general scheme of meaning (Kohler Riessman 1990). The narrative form of the accounts must be exam-ined with this in mind. The *manner of narrating* depicts the attempt to span the conflict between an action and the marital/life projects.

In the first quotation, Vladimir E describes his use of violence in terms of a desire to get his wife to stop "talking shit", and stresses that he did not mean to hurt her at all. In this way, he presents his action as something understandable, although not acceptable. Thus a possibility is created to span the conflict between the action and the marital and life projects. Pablo J's manner of narrating does not of-fer the same possibility. He presents the violence against the woman he loves, and lives with in a highly valued marriage, as something incomprehensible and despicable. "You sort of go crazy", Pablo J says, and cries.

I interpret my informants' agreeing to talk about the violent act as an urge to make sense of what happened, as an attempt to develop a *reasonable enough understanding* of the violent act. That is, an understanding that may bridge the conflict between violent action and marital/life projects in a reasonable enough manner. In a male perspective, a narrative form favoring words about *why* he acted as he did, served that purpose better than a form favoring words about *how* he did it. It is as though these men deem it possible for a reasonable enough understanding to contain a description of their good intentions (Vladimir E), or to involve total incomprehension (Pablo J).

In the women's accounts given soon after the violent act, I could trace their attempts to develop a reasonable enough understanding in their struggle for working at the experiences of threat to their life projects as represented by the violence. The women focused on the *consequences* of the act for them. The women talked about their fear of physical harm, their fear of being mentally or emotionally broken, and their attempts to protect themselves:

> I got so scared...I ran down to the laundry room and hid. Some weeks later, the same thing happened, but this time I ran out and called the police/.../ You know, sometimes I have been able to calm him down. Maybe I just didn't want to this time/.../ That would mean that I was giving in to him, and that would be the same as admitting that I had been wrong... so, it was not only to avoid losing the fight; it was also for my own self-respect. But this means that I am becoming more afraid; I don't know what he is liable to do. Whatever I do, it really shatters me. (Irene E, individual interview)

At a later point in the research process, the women's accounts changed and highlighted the conflict between the violent act and the joint marital project. But at the beginning, the matter of their own lives was, not surprisingly, in focus.

The use of a contrasting language

In texts on woman battering, surprisingly little attention has been given to how the men and the women perceive and label the violent events according to their gender. In other words, surprisingly few questions have been asked about how the women and men view the kind of incidents they have been involved in and instigated. The majority of texts on woman battering deal with the concept of "battering", as if there were a general understanding of the meaning and use of the concept. In my informants' narratives, this did not prove to be the case.

Thirteen of my male informants had been reported to the police, and their acts of violence were investigated under the crime caption "assault". In the remaining cases, the local social service bureau had captioned the events as "assault". Only five men used the word "assault" to describe the acts they had committed. Fourteen labelled the act as a part of a "fight"; one man called it "harassment" (Sw. "trakasseri"). The following description of "assault" represents a typical example of a male perception of the various kinds of violent acts:

> Assault, that's real hitting. But to call pushing an assault... that's ridiculous. If the police come, you go to jail in any case. They don't even need any witnesses; it's enough if the woman says that that's what happened. It's really horrible to call shoving an assault. I think most people would agree with me. If someone says: He beat me, then I think of real hitting, the worst stuff. Otherwise it's quarreling or fighting. People can get mean, and you may have to defend yourself. Most times, it's enough to draw the line, but you may have to strike out. Hell, the way people carry on... do you have to take that?...If you do, you'd end up like a bloody puppy-dog /.../ But it's not OK to keep slugging away after the other person has given up...some people would just keep on going, wouldn't even stop kicking. God damn! Now *that's* a real assault, and that's bad! Those types ought to be put away! (Vladimir E, individual interview)

The men classified the violent acts according to the *seriousness* of the violent attack as well as to the *degree of reciprocity between victim and attacker*. When a violent act was described as an assault by the men, serious violence had been committed and the attacker was clearly dominant in relation to his victim, and was thus in control of the situation.

Only five men used the word "assault" to describe the act they had committed. One man called his violent activity "harassment", a principally verbal aggressive act characterized by less serious physical violence. Fourteen of the men labelled the incident "a fight", a reciprocal activity with no clear distinction between "attacker" and "victim". Vladimir, in the example given above, explained how he viewed the difference between "assault" and "fight". He labelled what he had participated in as a "fight":

We have fights, sure. When she starts harping about something and doesn't stop, I get real down. Then we have an argument/../ First comes the screaming, back and forth, then maybe some plants go flying...but I don't call this assault. There was no hitting with fists or in the face...It was more like this...[acts out slaps and shoves]. It was just a reaction...you start shoving...react like a human being/.../ Maybe sometimes you spit in her face. (Vladimir E, individual interview)

In Vladimir's narrative, his emphasizing of *his wife's* "harping", as well as the "screaming back and forth" is an essential factor in his labeling of *his* violent actions as part of a "fight". Below is his wife Ingela's description of what he calls "fights":

The first time he hit me...yeah, it was when I was pregnant. But then he hit me carefully, because he was also real afraid of hurting me while I was pregnant. It was mostly what you'd call smacks. Like shoves and slaps. Then, after our daughter was born, it got worse. But he never keeps on hitting me after I'm down on the floor, like you read about. So maybe its not battering after all...But it is battering if you get hit so much that you are completely broken...terrified. (Irene E, individual interview)

According to my female informants, the primary feature of assault is the man's clear position of dominance in relation to the woman. In those cases where the man's dominance was not obvious, but instead where some form of reciprocity prevailed, a violent act could nevertheless be characterized as assault, if the woman was "broken" by the violent act. It was the *effect, more than the brutality* of what was done, as well as the *degree of reciprocity* between victim and attacker, that determined the female categorization of the violent act. The concept of effect here refers to how much the violence has affected the woman. In the words of the woman above, the crucial factor is whether or not she had been mentally or physically "broken" (Sw. "knäckt") by the violence.

The concept of effect was related to the seriousness of the violence in such a way that the risk of the woman being "broken" was greater if the violence was serious than if it was minor. According to the women, however, there was no simple correlation here. Even minor violence might have disastrous consequences for a woman. The following description represents a typical example of a female perception of "assault", focusing on the crucial concept of being "mentally broken" (Sw. "själsligt knäckt"):

He has a particular way of screaming, long and loud. He doesn't stop, just keeps at it for hours on end. I get so scared and can't tell what he's going to do. I try to avoid it in every way I possibly can. If I raise my voice, I just get more back. Same if I lower my voice and slip away. He usually says that my ways of avoiding fights all lead to more fighting./.../ He twists my nipples, he hits me in the face so that my glasses fly off and then I can't see anything. And the mean things he says shows his contempt: '...You disgust me, you bitch...now you are really going to get it...' That really gets to me, breaks me, not only physically, but also emotionally. (Kristina L, individual interview)

Only one woman used the word "fight" to describe the actual violent act, whereas the rest of the women labelled the violence they had been subjected to as "assaults".

Of all the violent acts that occur in marriages, the form of violence designated as assault is the most difficult to integrate into marital life. The concept of "integration" is used here to describe the process of continuing a marital relationship with violence as a component. The idea is not the acceptance of the violence, but rather the ability to remain in a relationship where such violent incidents have occurred and do occur.

"Assault" is the form of violence where the attacker exploits his dominant position in order to place the victim in an even more vulnerable position by causing fear, pain, and injury. It is the type of act that is in greatest contrast to that which is hoped for in terms of the love and care associated with marriage, according to the idea of "romantic love" as the base of marital life. To integrate a "fight" is much less of a problem. A "fight" is not as morally reprehensible as an "assault", since the responsibility for the incident is shared. The principle finding here is that the majority of women describe actions which are very difficult to integrate into a marriage, whereas the men see themselves as having committed acts less difficult to integrate. The men's designations for the acts reveal their perception of them as being compatible with marital life. The women's designations indicate the opposite.

Men talk about the violent incident: A controlled act

In the literature, the violent act has usually been described as an *impulsive* act that occurs because the man loses control and is overcome by his aggressive impulses (Schultz 1960; Snell, Rosenwald and Robey 1964; Faulk 1974; Cullberg 1984; Gondolf 1985; Homberger and Hastings 1986). An act of that kind, that exists beyond the realms of consciousness, is not easy to give an account of. Therefore,

I had expected my male informants to have difficulty in describing the violent events.

During the initial round of interviews, this expectation was fulfilled. When I asked the men to describe what had happened during the violent incident itself, the typical response was "and then it just went blank and I did not come to before I heard her screaming" or "I just blacked-out, and then she was on the floor bleeding". Such accounts triggered an image of men committing their violent acts in a state of total amnesia.

During the subsequent interviews, I decided to attempt to map out what had happened step-by-step. I sometimes confronted the men with their accounts of the violent act (for more about this methodological approach, see chapter 3). This approach proved quite useful. The accounts then changed character, as the violent act was presented as a conscious, controlled act, with clear rules as to the degree of violence permissible and an awareness of when these rules had been transgressed.

> *It* went too far the last time. Previously...yeah, I kicked her on the shoulder, I kicked her another time too. Since then, I haven't beaten her. But this time I *obviously* went too far. It seems I just stood there and beat on her./.../ I *must have* grabbed her by the throat and banged her head against the wall. *They found* strangle marks on her throat, but *I have no memory* of it. It's awful when she tells what happened. She thought her time had come. I had had quite a lot to drink and was undoubtedly rather smashed. Not until afterwards when I sat in jail did I find out what happened. I was shocked. (Hans A, individual interview)

When Hans A in this quotation describes actions which he claims constituted a violation of the rules ("It went too far the last time"), his language becomes vague. In his presentation, there is a certain degree of uncertainty as to whether the act's perpetrator and the narrative first-person is the same person. This separation of the narrative first-person and the subject of the act is typical for the *rhetorical form*, which is often adopted by the men when discussing the violent events.

Hans describes how he almost violated the rule that *marital violence against women may not be lethal or cause serious injuries.* During the incident in question, he had "had quite a lot to drink and was undoubtedly rather smashed". The significance of alcohol on one's ability to abide by this rule was recounted by all of the informants. In the six cases where serious violence occurred, four of the men were under the influence of alcohol; in the eleven cases of semi-serious violence, five of the men had been drinking; as had one of the men in the three cases of minor violence.

The men gave three reasons for why they used violence:

– they used violence *to put an end* to the verbal fight

– they used violence as *part* of the verbal fight.

– they used violence as a *reaction to earlier events* in the marriage.

"It was just stop it, stop talking shit"

In the quotation from the interview with Vladimir E that opened this chapter, he claimed to have hit his wife because he "just didn't want to hear any more". He "had heard enough", and wanted to stop her from "talking shit". Ten of the men made similar statements. They described how they used violence in order to put an end to the verbal fight, to prevent their wives' further rantings. In the following quotation, Per B describes how he used violence to prevent his wife Sonja from hurting their child:

> It would be wrong to say that we often fight. But when it happens, it's always the same thing/.../ Sonja can go around and work herself up about anything. It doesn't need to be about me, it can be about totally different things. So when she has been drinking... she gets all wound up and all her aggressions come out. It usually stops with her leaving and walking around to calm down. When she comes back, she says she's going to move out, and that she's taking the baby with her. I couldn't let that happen. I have to stop it, physically so to speak. That's when she jumps at me and starts fighting. It's at that point that I sometimes hit her to get her to calm down. (Per B individual interview)

In the following quotation, Refa D describes how he used violence to prevent his wife Fathima from hurting herself:

> **IP**: She's always sad. I try to help her. I call her three times a day, and when I come home, I always try to tell her how good dinner is. But she is so very homesick, and she is sad she doesn't have a good job. Soon she'll be unemployed again, after having had a temporary job for six months. Next month, she'll be unemployed /.../ Then we'll start fighting again... when we fought the last time she was so sad, she went to the police and reported me.
> **I**: Had you hit her then?
> **IP**: Nah, not hit her. But she thinks I have beaten her... she gets nervous and says really mean things. Then when I want to stop her.... she also

tears at herself when she gets nervous. She is very nervous and scratches herself. She has also hit herself.

I: She's hit herself?

IP: Yeah, she's done that also. I was in jail for a week. And she cried the whole time. But then in the courtroom, she said she wasn't mad at me. She said she cares about me./.../ When she gets that upset... last time she ran out... I was forced to stop her... I was scared she was going to hurt herself.

A common conception about wife battering is that the man has difficulty expressing himself verbally, and therefore starts throwing punches when the words fail him. What the ten men who claimed to have used violence in order to put an end to a verbal fight were saying was closer to the opposite: *They use their fists because they did not want to hear any more words*, not because they had run out of them. Stopping another human being by means of physical violence is a well-tried, effective, and not very sophisticated means of enforcing silence:

It's when she's been drinking and gets aggressive that I hit her, 'coz that's the only way I can get her to keep quiet/.../ One midsummer, we had a beauty of a fight, and Nina got more and more aggressive. I had tried to stop her, even our friends tried to stop her. But she wouldn't ease up. She yelled and shouted, but then when she pulled my hair and scratched me, that was the limit. I threw her out and gave her a good beating/.../ Sometimes I get a little high from one glass of wine and I hit her, but not always. And I have always known what I was doing. Mostly I have just hit her with an open hand, a few times with a fist. But I have never used any weapon or kicked her. She only understands when I beat it into her. That's the only way she understands that she has done something wrong and that she can't keep doing it/.../ After I've hit her, then she runs to the neighbors and screams and shouts that she has been beaten and reports me to the police. The laws in this society allow a woman to act any way and say anything. When the man reacts, then it becomes illegal/.../ The only thing I want is a little peace and quiet and to be able to talk things over without her claws coming out and her throwing back everything I've said to her in my face, only twice as hard. (Fredrik P, individual interview)

In this quotation, Fredrik argues in a way typical of the accounts of the violent incident as being aimed at stopping the woman in some way. He regards his action as morally acceptable in that Nina's behavior had been indefensible and had to be stopped. In this way, the violent incident is portrayed as a joint enterprise. Fredrik further supports his way of reasoning by referring to the fact that his perception of her needing to be stopped was shared by many, and that all alternative methods of dealing with the situation short of violence had already been exhausted. Implied in this way of accounting for the violent incident, is the apprehension that in a situation like this Fredrik's efforts to gain control are not only defensible, but called for.

Fredrik's account differs in one important way from the others where men describe stopping their women with violence: He does not condemn his action. The majority of men, regardless of the reason for their use of violence, denounce the use of violence per se, as seen in the quotation below from Hans:

> It's awful to think about. I must have hit her hard, with my fist. I think she ended up with a concussion. That must have happened when I banged her head against the wall. It's awful, oh God! (Hans A, individual interview)

As a well-tried means for enforcing the subordination of others, the use of violence offered these men the best option for achieving what they wanted. They "didn't want to hear any more". They "had heard enough". And they beat their wives into silence.

"It escalates and turns into bigger and bigger fights"

Eight of the men allude to a blurry transition from the verbal fight into the violent incident. As the verbal aggression escalates, the physical violence begins. Kristina L. describes how such a violent incident evolves:

> He twists my nipples, he hits me in the face so that my glasses fly off and then I can't see anything. And he shows his contempt through the mean things he says: '...You disgust me, you bitch...now you are really going to get it...' (Kristina L, individual interview)

In order to understand the function of violence in these cases, we need to recapitulate what the verbal aggressive act looks like:

> – the interaction follows a stereotypical pattern of attack and counterattack.

> – the communicational sequence accelerates, so that one complaint is met with a still more serious counter complaint, one insult is met with a still worse insult.

– at the center of interest are the *actors themselves.* Both partners strive to gain an advantage over the other, not by attempting to outclass or surpass the other, and thereby using their own merits to assure themselves of first place, but rather to gain the advantage by *belittling* their counterpart.

The strategy in the verbal fight phase of "belittling" the other party and of "communicating worthlessness", entails a series of attempts to cause narcissistic harm through verbal attacks. When the man uses physical violence as part of a verbal fight, he uses violence as an additional means for attaining this goal. He hopes to get the woman to act differently, namely, to do what he wants, and he hopes to prevent his loss of the initiative in the discussion. Carl-Magnus L, the husband of the above quoted Kristina, describes this as follows:

> She is capable of risking everything for the sake of a completely crazy discussion. She backs herself into a corner and then tries to defend the most absurd position. In an effort to put me down, she can shut herself off, like in a daze. Then there is no more any contact, nothing to work out, all promises forgotten. Or she can respond to everything with totally irrelevant associations, so that only an absurd discussion can result. In this way, I can never get or keep the upperhand. *It's only an illusion that we discuss what I bring up. In reality, she controls the whole discussion.* This type of dishonesty builds an enormous amount of pressure inside of me, so it grows, and leads to bigger and bigger fights. Sometimes we go on like that for three-four hours. (Carl-Magnus L, initial individual interview)

What Carl-Magnus is attempting to do here is not to put an end to the verbal fight, but rather to *continue it in another form.* He wants to interrupt the symmetrically escalating interaction and replace it with a complementary one, with him in the position of control. The men who used violence in order to put an end to a verbal fight basically had the same goal of replacing the symmetrically escalating interaction with a complementary interplay with them in the dominant and the women in the subordinate position, but for the simultaneous purpose of ending the verbal fight.

As already stated, the use of violence is a well-tried means for enforcing the subordination of others. It is not only effective at stopping another human being, and preventing her from certain actions, it is also a very effective means of causing narcissistic harm. (About battered women's low self-esteem, see further Walker 1979; Pagelow 1981; Araldsen and Clasen 1983; Christensen 1984). Ulla expresses this as follows:

> If he had loved me enough, he wouldn't have done this. You start feeling so worthless. I think it's that that gets me thinking, 'Ah, I can't go to the store with a black eye'. Others will start saying to themselves, 'Ah, he can't love you.' That's how you think. That's why you don't want to let anybody know about what happened. (Ulla A, individual interview)

A violent act that is a component of a verbal fight has no end in the way that a violent act constituting the end of an argument does. Subsequently, the violence in the verbal fight is frequently very serious. None of the eight cases where the men claimed to have resorted to violence as part of a verbal fight have involved minor violence. The violence was very serious in one case, serious in two, and semi-serious in five cases. "He stops when he's totally exhausted, or he asks me to get out of there because he's afraid of losing control and hitting me too much", Kristina comments about how the violent act stops.

Pablo J, who was quoted earlier in this chapter, was responsible for one of the cases of serious violence. He describes below the context in which this violence took place:

> When I got home that day, I started fighting with my wife. It happens that she lies to me. She does it rather often, even if there's no reason to. We have tried to talk this through because it's a big problem for me. But it doesn't work. When I have been drinking, all this comes back to me. And then... I know that I have messed this up... She lied to me something terrible... I mistrust her about everything... I have got to make her tell me the truth... I get so upset... I couldn't stand all the lies. (Pablo J, individual interview)

Pablo has one way of viewing the subject they are discussing, his wife Angela has another. At the time of the above quoted situation, they were short of money. She could not find any particular explanation for this – they simply had used more money than they could afford. He had a plausible explanation, however: she had supported her relatives, something that he had forbidden her to do. She maintained her position; he perceived it as a denial, as a lie.

Like Carl-Magnus in the previous quotation, Pablo did not use violence as an attempt to put an end to the verbal fight, but rather to force it to continue in an other form. Pablo wants his wife to start "telling the truth", and then he will stop hitting her and attacking her verbally. He never attains his goal. When morning comes, he falls asleep from total exhaustion. His wife Angela leaves the apartment and takes the children to their day-care center, where the staff calls an ambulance.

"I wanted to do something just as horrid as she had done"

In two cases, the violent incident was not preceded by a verbal fight. In both cases, the marriage was in the process of breaking up. In Katrin and Hector C's case, minor violence occurred when he came to meet his daughter. The most serious incident occurred just prior to my contact. Hector had waited for Katrin in the subway, and when she arrived, he attacked her from behind, hitting her in the face and dragging her by the hair towards their previously shared apartment. During the telephone conversation I have with Hector, he explains that he was exploding with rage. He wanted to show Katrin and the world that she "couldn't treat me like dirt".

In the previous chapter, I described the pre-history of one of these cases, that of Lisa and Ismeth Q's earlier marital life. One Saturday afternoon, Ismeth came to call on his daughter. Lisa was serving him coffee when it happened:

> I had gotten the idea from a movie. It was about a man, a respected corporate executive, who was constantly terrorized by his wife. Finally, he couldn't take it any more. He forced her to go outside naked, so people could see her and be shamed in front of everyone/.../ When I got to Lisa's, I can't explain how filled with hate I was. If you haven't felt like this, you can't understand. I had a big knife with me. I never intended to use it, but I needed it to threaten her/.../ At first everything went well. I forced her to take off her clothes. But then nothing went the way it was supposed to. I couldn't get her out of the house. She didn't say anything, she just didn't move. I didn't know what to do. I thought I wanted to do something just as horrid as she had done... I intended to screw her... I got her down on the floor by threatening her with the knife... we had some sort of sex... [voice got weaker and weaker]... the worst thing is that Anna was in the kitchen and watched everything... (Ismeth Q, individual interview)

Lisa recounts the same incident in the following way:

> We drank coffee. Suddenly, he gets up, goes out, and when he comes back he's carrying a big knife in his hand. He held it up to my face and threatened to kill me. I remember thinking I had to get help and I tried to get out in the hall. He came after me... he grabbed at my clothes... and pulled my hair... shoved me. I was bruised all over... the whole time the knife... he didn't say so much... He [sniffles] forced me to take off all my clothes... then he pulled down his pants and pushed me down so I would suck him [cries]/.../ I don't know for how long... Then he forced me to lean forward, forced himself into me from behind... the whole time he had the knife against my leg. It was horrible/.../ If you haven't been through something like that, you can't understand. I think I was totally

stiff, like cold. I thought he was going to kill me. And the whole time I could see Anna standing in the kitchen. I think she went and hid... Suddenly he stopped and said something like 'now I've gotten what I needed'. Then he pulled up his pants and left. (Lisa Q, individual interview)

Ismeth did not attain his principal goal. He did not force her to disgrace herself in front of the neighbors. He degraded her in his presence and part of the degradation was witnessed by their daughter. He did not achieve the feeling of redress that he sought. It was not even a matter of course anymore that she was the degraded person, and not himself. Shortly after, he was convicted of aggravated rape and assault in two cases.

Lisa and Ismeth, were the only couple who told about sexual attacks in connection with the battering. My material provides no evidence which would support the findings from other studies that woman battering is not infrequently accompanied by sexual abuse (Lundgren 1985). On the other hand, my material provides no evidence which would refute these findings, either.

Women tell about the violent incident: An act with severe consequences

My female informants' accounts deal foremost with what the men had done to them and what the consequences of these actions were. The women talk about events that were extremely physically painful for them, without ever explicitly talking about pain. Pain is ubiquitous in their accounts, but it is never named. This absence of pain amazed me. I think it is worth reflecting on.

"Physical pain has no voice", Scarry states in her comprehensive theoretical work, *The Body in Pain* (1985). When one listens to an account of another person's physical pain, the events happen within the interior of that person's body. Thus, when a person speaks about his or her "own physical pain" and about "another person's physical pain", these may seem to be two wholly distinct orders of events. Whatever it is that pain achieves, it achieves it in part through the impossibility of sharing it, and it ensures this unshared nature through its resistance to language (Scarry 1985). The impossibility of sharing this experience with another human being reflects a linguistic deficiency, according to Scarry, who quotes Virginia Woolf: "English", Woolf writes, "which can express the thoughts of Hamlet and the tragedy of Lear has no words for the shiver or the headache...The merest schoolgirl when she falls in love has Shakespeare or Keats to speak her mind for her, but let a sufferer try to describe a pain in his head to a doctor and language at once runs dry'' (Woolf 1967 in Scarry 1985).

True for the headache, Woolf's account is even more dramatically true for the severe and prolonged pain that may accompany the violence a woman is subjected to by her husband.

Moreover, it was difficult but still possible for my female informants to find some verbal expression for the *fear* for what their men had done to them, and how they had tried to *escape* the violence:

> He came home late that night and started fighting... I think it was because I had reported him to the police for assault a few weeks earlier... He said that that had been really stupid, that the children would end up in the middle, if I stopped them from living a normal family life. But I can't remember too well. It's always like that when he hits me a lot/.../ He hit me in the face with his fists... he kicked me all over my body. I was bleeding a lot and I was crying and begged him to stop, 'stop, stop'. After a while, he stopped and I went into the bathroom to wash up. He came in there and tried to hit me with his fists. I remember that blood got splattered on the wall, because when he finally finished, he told me to clean up in the bathroom. Then he went in there and wiped it up himself. After that, he left the apartment and was gone for about an hour/.../ When he came home again, he had a friend with him. They sat and drank in the kitchen. When his friend left, he started accusing me of having destroyed our family life and started hitting me again. I got really scared 'coz he didn't usually hit me this much. I tried to go out in the hall. The children woke up and started crying. That's what got him to calm down/.../ I think it was morning by then, since he said we were all going to go to the police and report what happened. He couldn't take it any more. We started getting dressed. Then when we were ready he changed his mind. So he hit me again... and then he went and laid down. He must have been tired, because he fell asleep. I left with the children and went to the day-care center. I got help there. (Angela J, individual interview)

The women described the violent incident often in terms of a specific referential content, that of their individual life projects. They talked about the men's violence and then about how it had caused fear and depression in their lives:

> He got so mad. First he started harping about something. Then I answered him back a little... then he hit me... beat me good... I was one big bruise. I was bleeding, and I had black and blue marks /.../ It's so awful. I got so upset and sad. Why does he do this to me? (Sonja B, individual interview)

> He never kicks me. He only hits me with his hands. Against my head.

Wherever. It's difficult remembering everything, for when it happens, I get so nervous. I get so afraid/.../ I am very sad, very pessimistic. I am so disappointed, because everything has turned out the opposite of what I had hoped for. When I was little... you know, I dreamed. Those type of dreams young girls dream/.../ I was very good. I was one girl among six brothers. I was always happy, and I had every chance. But it turned out the opposite of what I had dreamed about. Had I known then what I know now, I would never have moved in with him. I have lost everything because of him....

I feel real bad sometimes. I was real good this morning, but then in the afternoon, I felt like I was going to faint. I don't know what happens, I get so dizzy. It's hard. This type of thing makes you sad. I who have always been so strong, gone around, made people look at me. Now I can't cope with anything. I have been through every type of examination, but they don't find anything wrong with me. I feel like I am going to die. I dream about dying. It hurts so bad. (Fathima D, individual interview)

Having different perceptions of the purpose of the violent act

The difference between the men's and the women's way of recounting what happened makes the concept of "purpose" crucial for understanding how the man and the woman make sense of the violent incident. But it is also crucial for understanding the type of marriage the violent marriage has evolved into.

Despite the fact that the man and the woman are actors on the same stage and are part of an incident that they by and large describe in similar ways – a pre-history, the course of the event, the role of alcohol – the experience of the act leads to at least two different perceptions of the purpose of it. Two different understandings of the act also result.

The man identifies his own purpose as that of *influencing the woman*, since it is necessary for him to prevent her from injuring herself or someone else or to get her to act differently. Based on her perspective of the consequences of his violence on her life, she identifies his purpose as that of *wanting to harm her*. She can describe the situation in which the purpose applies, and she can describe how it happened. But in the perspective of their joint marital project, she is unable to understand it.

By citing the purpose of his own action as that of influencing the woman, the man, on the other hand, makes his action comprehensible to himself. These divergent perceptions of the man's purpose are reflected in the differences in the terminology that I have discussed above, where the man prefers to talk about "fights" and to stress the reciprocity in the action, and where the woman talks about "assaults" and emphasizes the one-sidedness of the action.

If we continue this discussion about the divergent perceptions of the man's intentions, the issue arises as to what *type of responsibility* the man and the woman consider appropriate in relation to the man's use of violence.

As I have noted earlier, in daily life, we often view our feelings as reactions which result from provocation. We use expressions such as "you make me mad" or "I think that it is her boss's dissatisfaction with her that has made her so desperate". When we make such statements, we also make the judgement that it is the object of our anger and not we ourselves that are responsible for our anger. With this type of argumentation, an extreme position as to responsibility for one's own actions is to focus on the condition in which an individual (A) finds herself, and to hold the person (B) who caused her to be in such a condition responsible for all ensuing events.

The opposite extreme position focuses on the condition an individual (B) has placed another person (A) in, and where the individual (B) who placed the other person in that condition takes responsibility for the other person's reaction. In accordance with this way of allocating responsibility, A can act in such a way that makes B sad or upset. When B expresses these feelings, A becomes sad and upset, which in turn causes B to apologize for hurting and upsetting A. Here, B puts the blame on herself.

Both of these extreme interpretations of the allocation of responsibility when individuals act in an interplay situation make it impossible for the parties to see the purposes of their actions in relation to one another. Furthermore, if they are unable to do this, they will also have difficulty in dealing with conflicts.

In a conflict between two individuals, the focus is on the difference between them: He wants one thing and she another. This difference creates a chasm between them. In order to be able to bridge this gap, they have to become more alike in terms of the closeness, which means coming out of themselves for a moment, without this implying a denial or an attempt to obliterate the boundary between them as individuals.

If one or both parties in a conflict adopt one of the extreme positions outlined above, the conflict will cease to be about differences. In the one extreme position, the parties suddenly find themselves in a situation where it is a question of ending the painful situation they find themselves in, by holding one of the parties responsible. In the other extreme position, it is a matter of, at all costs, compensating the other for the situation she/he was in. Human beings have the tendency to adopt one or the other of these two extreme positions. Some behave like external creditors, constantly placing demands on others and constantly seeking someone to take the responsibility. Others are like permanent debtors and behave as if they were burdened down by constant guilt or by continually neglecting their duty. These individuals are always seeking something they ought to have taken responsibility for long ago.

The men's accounts reveal an aptitude for adopting the extreme position that allows others, in these cases their wives, to take responsibility for the painful condition they are in as well as for the actions they committed in order to put a stop to this condition. From the women's accounts about the violent incident, it is difficult to determine their stance on the issue of responsibility. Their accounts are future-oriented and focus on descriptions of the consequences of the incidents, and not on who has responsibility for the emergence of the situation. Nevertheless, I will return to the question of the women's propensity to take responsibility, when the sequel of the violent act is discussed in the next chapter. In some types of accounts originating from the sequel of the violent incident, the woman and the man quite clearly make a joint project out of exculpating the man from the responsibility for his actions.

Does the man achieve his purpose? The informants' accounts indicate both affirmative and negative answers to this question. Affirmative, because the interplay in the current violent situation is altered to the advantage of the man, where he can retain the dominant position and control over the situation by means of relegating the woman to the subordinate position. Negative, because his violence reinforces the form of interplay that constitutes the pre-history that he considered unbearable. Negative also because by committing a questionable marital action, he places himself in a vulnerable position. The consequences of this is the topic of the next chapter.

A second note on social order

Here, it should be borne in mind that a prominent feature of the social process underway during the pre-history referred to as a "verbal fight", was described as "the endeavor to question the status of the other person, and to demote him or her to a lower ranking". The social order produced by this activity could be suitably described as a hierarchical organization of the marital project.

The *central issue* of the narratives of the pre-history, can be concluded as A making a request of B to change action, a request reflecting a certain understanding of rights on behalf of A, and obligations on behalf of B. When B refuses the request, this refusal reflects a denial of A's rights and B's obligations. This issue of requests and refusals is strongly associated with a dispute over rights and obligations reflecting a certain understanding of the participants' social status, or rather a *conflict* around this understanding: both parties make claims on the dominant position.

Looking more closely at this understanding one might conclude that *rights* in my informants' view are exclusively connected to the position of *dominance*, while *obligations* are exclusively connected to *subordination*. What is conspicuous by its absence are the other two conceivable combinations: the one where a superior position implies certain obligations, and the other where a subordinate position brings certain rights to its possessor.

The hierarchical social order of my informants' marital projects never seemed to be called into question, in spite of all the dissatisfaction expressed. On the contrary, the repeated efforts to question the status of the other person seemed to reinforce the hierarchical order. The defense of rights and the struggle for status then set the stage for the man's physical violent action. The man's violent actions were found when the sequence of verbal aggressive speech acts led in a direction where 1) speech needed to be stopped, according to his judgement 2) speech was emphasized or strengthened by the violent action.

How distant is the idea of "romantic love" here, how inaccessible the intense wishes for reconciliation and belongingness. How easy to be successful in endeavors of stopping another person by use of violent means. How easy to be successful in efforts to emphasize a certain social status by the use of physical violence, how reinforcing for a hierarchical social order. What an absolute failure when it comes to the gaining of another person's love, when it comes to the gaining of understanding for one's needs and efforts.

The importance of previous experience of violence

My informants revealed quite varied experiences of violence in their childhood homes. Four of the men and five of the women described themselves as having been "spoiled" during their childhood. This conversation in a joint interview with Victor (V) and Maria F. (M) recounts Victor's upbringing:

M: Yeah, he was really spoiled. He told me how if it was raining outside, his mother kept him home from school. Isn't that right Victor? Your mother told me herself.

V: Yeah, yeah [laughs]. They would do anything for me.

Four of the men and three of the women had been seriously battered as children. Two men and three women described their childhood as "unsettled", "violent". They grew up in families where the father had been an alcoholic. They had been hit without calling it battering, and some of them had seen their mothers beaten. Four men and four women claimed to have had a "tough" background, characterized by a lack of money and a "rigid" father. Six of the men and five of the women described their childhood as "normal", "not special in any sense", and where violence consisted of "the occasional spanking".

To my question about the significance of their earlier experiences of violence for what was happening now, the "spoiled" women all replied that they could never have dreamed that they would have been beaten, and that this is why they became so afraid, so upset, and so condemning:

> I was never hit at home, not as much as a slap from my parents. I think that that's why I react so strongly. The way I was brought up, you could get angry, but not hit. It just wasn't done. I think it is so wrong. (Irene E, joint interview)

The "spoiled" men liked having been cherished as children, and would like this to continue:

> I waited for a long time to get married... I had my ideals... I was looking for something like what I was used to at home. My father came home to dinner on the table and all that. Then when I started getting to the age that I could imagine getting married... it wasn't like what I expected. The girls had become freer and hadn't grown up like I had at all. I would know ... [laughs]... when they couldn't even boil water for tea. They were out the door immediately! With Sonja, I could see at once that she was different! (Per B, joint interview)

There were two discernible patterns among my informants who had been beaten as children with regard to their understanding of the violence they had been subjected to now as adults, or the violence they commit. These patterns can be designated *submission* and *protest*. The following quotation from the interviews with Viveka and Nina may serve as examples of how two women who were both severely beaten as children developed very dissimilar patterns of understanding:

I have been beaten so much that I think there must be something wrong with me. I have been beaten so much and been through so much that I don't think very many others could have had the same experience... I got hit a lot as a kid, I think 'coz I caused trouble. After I turned twelve, I wasn't lively any more.... By then I had become a person who apologized for being alive, sort of like that/.../ It's hard living with myself nowadays... I hate it when it's messy and unfinished... My whole life is unfinished, but I don't do anything about it... I even admire Adam for putting up with me. (Viveka N, individual interview)

IP: It's also a fact that Hanna [her mother, author's note] and I have fought as long as I can remember.
I: You mean physical fighting?
IP: Yeah, ugly fistfights. We threw things at each other, and when I was little, my mother pounded me black and blue. It was like that the whole time. She hit me in the face with the dishrag, she beat me with a stick. But she couldn't get the better of me. She found out once that I was scared of the dark, so she starting locking me in the broom closet/.../ I think I was mad all the time. I was such a brat that no one could handle me/.../ I don't know, ...I'm the type that can never forget a wrong. I don't know whether Fredrik could continue, but I can't. Why is everything so hard to forget? It must be that our problems are mostly wounds that don't heal. (Nina P, joint interview)

In the accounts of men who had been beaten as children, any clear reference to the submission theme is missing, but there are different degrees of references to protest:

Normally, it was just grin and bear it. The first blows were always the worst. Then you started getting numb, and then you might as well keep quiet. Sometimes I thought about what I could do, but always realized there was nothing to do, that I just had to stick it out/.../ For some reason, both my sister and I were picked on real bad at school. I was small, so they figured I was just a dumb, little jerk. I didn't like to fight, I had had enough of that at home. But I did try to give as good as I got and to protect myself. So, I understood early on that one day I would be strong enough that no one could bully me. Nina usually says that my whole life is one big act of revenge/.../ Last time my father hit me was when I was fifteen. He tried to cream me... I punched him back and left him lying on the hall floor. (Fredrik P, joint interview)

Have you ever seen a pressure cooker? That's me. A ridiculously nice guy who never causes trouble. But it bubbles away inside of me until it boils over. (Birger S, individual interview)

My informants possessed quite varied experiences of violence ranging from both spouses being severely beaten in their childhood (Nina and Fredrik P), to neither of the spouses having experienced family violence (Maria and Victor F). From my informants' accounts, I learned the following about the relationship between previous and current experiences of violence within the family:

> – A man can batter and a woman can be battered within a marriage without either partner having previous experiences of violence. "Prior knowledge" is not required, either for the victim or for the perpetrator.
> – Women without the experience of violence in their original families consistently condemn their husbands' use of violence.
> – People can make sense of their previous experiences in different ways, along a declining scale from an acceptance of the violence as something "that just is", to something one strongly condemns, "never more will this happen".

Witnesses to violence – the children

Marital woman battering is an act that takes place in the couple's home usually without outsiders present. At the same time, the couple's home is their children's childhood home. From among the 141 police reports, 103 of the couples had a total of 122 children living at home. Twelve of the couples had no children, and for 26 couples, there was no information about this. Seventy-eight of the children were 0–6 years old, 26 were 7–12 years old, and 18 were 13–19 years old. Corresponding figures for my informant couples were 19 children 0–6 years, four children 7–12 years, and six children 13–19 years old.

In 69 percent of the police reports which indicated that the couple had children, it was noted that the children had been present during the assault. Since the majority of the families had children of ages when they are in or near the home when the parents are not at work, it is reasonable to assume that the children in these families had been at home.

In 67 percent of the cases where the children had been present, the child had seen the mother seriously beaten. In 35 percent of these cases, the child had heard the mother seriously verbally threatened. In another 25 percent of the cases, the children had seen the mother beaten with an instrument or other weapon.

If I had spoken to a group of my informants' children, I would undoubtedly have heard entirely different accounts from those of their parents'. The children's accounts would be determined by *the position* the children found themselves in during the violent act. The man's position was characterized by the fact that he was the perpetrator of the violence, and the woman's by the fact that she was the victim of it. What characterized the children's position?

In the heading of this section, I called the children the witnesses of the violence. The children are neither perpetrators nor direct recipients of the violence committed. But the children are not really witnesses in the typical sense of the word either, namely, that of an outside observer. It would be psychologically impossible for these children to be outside observers to events that are a part of their living environment. In this sense, they are "indirect victims of the violence", because they are in an anguish-filled situation that they have not themselves chosen, nor are responsible for. They are not outsiders, but rather "participatory" witnesses, since they are compelled to react in some way to the living environment they are in. Thus, the children's position is not determined once and for all. According to my understanding, it is also determined by the *method they develop to deal with* the violent act.

When I read the police reports and attempted to interpret how the children described in these reports dealt with the violent events in their living environments, I discovered a common denominator in the *degree of responsibility* the children felt for the violent act. The degree of responsibility could fall into three categories:

(1) In 54 of the cases, it is noted that the children *tried to escape from* the situation by remaining as passive as possible. They sat crying and frightened and watched what was going on, or they ran into an adjoining room and put their hands over their ears. A seven-year-old girl usually fainted from fear. A seven-month baby girl lay in her crib in the living room when an explosive fight broke out. It ended with the mother getting beaten and landing on top of the little girl. A four-year-old girl sat weeping in her mother's lap as the father threatened with a knife. A woman sat bleeding on the bed with her one-year-old held close to her. Nowhere is it noted how the presence of these children affected the situation.

Unborn children represent a very special situation. In five cases, there are entries indicating that the woman was assaulted during her pregnancy. In one of these cases, the father clearly expressed his repugnance at the thought of the child and wanted the woman to have an abortion.

(2) In 23 cases, it was noted that the children *actively intervened* to get the father to stop hitting. The children often succeeded. In some cases, the children's intervention resulted in their getting beaten as well. A seven-year-old girl witnessed how her father was trying to choke her mother. The girl forced her way in between her

parents, and begged and pleaded for her father to spare her mother. A nine-year-old girl saw her father hitting her mother and threatening to kill her. The mother cried out to the girl to fetch help. The girl was very upset and ran out. On her way out, she kicked her father on the leg.

The older the children in the intervening group, the more active their interventions. A 17-year-old witnessed how his father threatened to kill his mother with an empty bottle. He stepped between them and twisted the bottle out of his father's hand. A 16-year-old girl heard her parents fighting in the next room, as had happened many times before. She knew that her mother was going to get beaten up this time as well. She decided that it was time for this to be stopped, for good. She called the police. The arrival of the police calmed her father down, which observation the policeman wrote down in his notebook and prepared to leave. The girl became desperate and described everything her father had done and tried to convince the police to take him in and interrogate him. Finally, she succeeded. The father was later prosecuted and sentenced for his violence.

(3) A couple of the children behaved in a way that could be described as *indirect attempts* to influence the situation. When their parents started fighting, these children would start whining or fighting, get demanding, becoming aggressive or troublesome in some manner. As a result of this, the parents' attention would focus on the child – and not seldom their rage as well.

To be indirect victims of violence due to one's attempts to escape a situation implies living with an overwhelming sense of powerlessness. A six-year-old boy described his world like a world at war, where the outcome is determined in advance. Everything is total, closed, and unchangeable. A little girl hid behind the clothes in the hallway when her beloved father seriously battered her mother. He was sentenced to a long prison sentence. Her parents separated, and her father disappeared from her life. She told people that her father was dead. The man who was in prison had her father's name, but it was another man, not her father.

To live as a direct observer can also have the opposite effect. The child is put into a position of power, but a position of power which entails an unavoidable responsibility: my parents cannot cope with this, so I must deal with it. To be weak is an impossibility, dangerous. If the child "fails", this will lead to guilt feelings. Even a child who "succeeds" can be afflicted by guilt feelings: "Why didn't I intervene sooner?" The 16-year-old girl above told the police that she bitterly regretted not informing them sooner. She blamed herself that the battering had gone so far. After the trial she also said: "I was forced to do it, but for the rest of my life, I have to live with my guilt for sending my father to prison''.

I would like to point out one final essential factor in the way in which children are affected by the battering of their own mothers. Apparently, it is not only the violent acts in themselves, but also the long-term consequences of these acts for the women that are significant for the children's living environments. In 49 percent of the cases where the children witnessed the violence, there were notations that their mothers had developed mental problems as a result of the violence. It is reasonable to assume, that these children would have had a more burdensome childhood than those children whose mothers did not develop psychological problems to the extent they were noted in the records. (For further discussion, see Christensen 1990; and Jaffe et al. 1990).

The termination of the violent incident

When the man's purpose with the violent act is to stop the woman in some way, his use of violence ceases when he ''attains'' his goal. When the violent act constitutes a part of a verbal fight that the man wants to gain control over – not primarily to put an end to – there is no clear-cut end to the violent act. ''He must have been tired, since he fell asleep'' (Angela J, individual interview); ''Sometimes he yells at me to go, so he won't be able to hit me too much'' (Kristina L, individual interview) are examples of descriptions of how these types of violence end. In cases where the man claims that it was necessary for him to put a stop to the ''fight'' the couple have been having, and which does not lead to serious injuries, six of the couples remain at home together after the violent act ends.

Eight of the women left home after the violent incident which brought them into this study. All of these women described this particular incident as assault, claim to have been seriously injured, or to have been afraid of being harmed. Six men left home at the end of the violent act. What these men have in common is that they live in marriages where there is disagreement about the basic organization of the marital project and where the relationship is moving towards dissolution.

Accounts of the violent incident – a summary

An initial central observation upon reading the accounts of the violent incidents was that the men and women *defined* what could be counted as violence and *described* the actual violent incidents entirely differently.

The women defined both that which they perceived as violence and the actual violent incidents they were subjected to in terms of the *consequences* the men's actions had had for them, such as *fear* and *physical injuries*.

The men, on the other hand, tended to define the violence in part along a continuum with the poles reflecting the *degree of reciprocity* between victim and attacker, and in part based on the *function* filled by the violence. Different types of functions were found in the men's accounts:

> as a *part* of the verbal fight; something that leads to a violent escalation and very serious consequences for the woman. A violent outburst serving this function with no natural end, in contrast to the violent outburst that is a means for *ending* the verbal fight. The violent outburst can also be revenge for previously perceived injustices, or a *reaction* to a separation, an action that appears to be a desperate attempt to 'fight his way back'.

The violent incident reinforced the hierarchical social order, containing a dominant and subordinate position, that was revealed, refuted and reconstituted by means of turn taking during the "verbal fight" of the pre-history. By using violent means the man gained the dominant position in the hierarchy.

Previous experiences of violence seem to be of significance for both the men's and the women's interpretations of the violent incident. This came across clearest in the women's accounts. A general characteristic of these accounts is that the women who lack any prior experience of family violence have extremely negative reactions to the violent incident and become quite afraid. Those women with some experience of violence tend to react either with *submission* or *protest*.

The correlation between a person's previous violent experiences and current ones does not seem to be particularly strong. A man can obviously batter a woman with or without previous experience of violence. "Prior knowledge" may be present, but is not required, either for the victim or for the perpetrator.

7

The Aftermath

Introduction

The immediate consequences of the man's violence for the seriously battered women included a visit to a hospital or other medical centers. The immediate consequences of the man's violence for the seriously battering men included being arrested by the police, in some cases leading to a trial and conviction.

Only rarely in cases of medium-serious or minor battering did the violent incident lead to such palpable interventions by the "surroundings" for the purpose of protecting and assisting the woman or holding the man accountable. The immediate consequence of such incidents varied from total silence between the spouses, followed by one or both falling into bed exhausted, to one or both temporarily leaving home for a few hours or days. At this point, some of the women reported the violence to the police. In cases of medium-serious or minor violence, these reports did not generally lead to any direct or extensive reaction by the police. Not infrequently, they were instead "shelved" awaiting assignment to an investigator, which was followed by a slow process of inquiry, which not often led to the case being dropped due to lack of evidence.

The accounts of the violent acts underlying the previous chapter were obtained soon after the violent incident occurred. Several of the initial individual interviews took place when the spouses were apart, either because the man was in jail, or had left home and was temporarily living with friends or relatives, or because the woman and the children had obtained a temporary placement through the social authorities or were living at a women's shelter or with relatives.

The interviews containing the account that forms the basis of this chapter occurred after a certain period of time had lapsed. The majority of couples were once again living under the same roof. The time that had passed since the initial interviews about the violent incident ranged from weeks to months. During this period of time, the two parties had begun a process of integration/dissociation that I will discuss in terms of the *aftermath period*.

In the following, I propose to describe the aftermath phase as the phase following the violent incident, during which the man and the woman, jointly or separately, develop an understanding of what had happened. That is, they reach conclusions about the effect of the violent incident on their joint marital project as well as on their individual life projects. Furthermore, the aftermath is the phase during which the woman and man decide to continue the marriage or to separate.

The nature of the narrative accounts, on which the analytical work in this chapter is based differs somewhat from the narratives of the previous chapters. The analysis of the pre-history and violent incident was founded on narratives told in retrospect, as I asked my informants to tell me about what had happened in the past. The analysis of the aftermath is based on narratives told in prospect, that is, the interviewing continued over a two-year period of time, in order to follow the development of my informants' means of making sense of the earlier violent outbursts.

To analyze narrative accounts of the aftermath phase

Classifying by content

The classic article "Accounts" by Lyman and Scott (1968) serves as a good starting point for my analysis. In their article, Lyman and Scott proposed that when an untoward or unanticipated behavior has occurred, a gap arises between the action and the expectation. The agent therefore tends to account for this action in such a way that this gap is spanned. Accounts that serve this purpose can be classified according to content, such as under "excuses" and "justifications" (see further Austin 1990), each with its own sub-types (Lyman and Scott 1968).

Excuses and justifications constitute socially approved terminology which neutralize an act or its consequences, when one or both are questioned. "Justifications" are accounts in which one *accepts responsibility* for the act in question, but *denies* the pejorative qualities associated with it. Lyman and Scott exemplify this by telling about a soldier who admits to killing but who denies the immorality of the act, since he had killed an enemy "deserving of his fate". "Excuses", on the other hand, are accounts in which one admits that the act in question is bad, but *denies responsibility,* since the act instead of being undertaken entirely voluntarily, was committed under some kind of compulsion, accident, or biological drive (Lyman and Scott 1968).

Following in Lyman and Scott's footprints, I began my analytical work by classifying the accounts according to content. I then identified two types of accounts: *neutralizations* and *rejections,* each with its own subtypes.

The accounts I classified as neutralizations were accounts in which the man *indirectly admitted his involvement* in the violent incident by dissociating himself from it, but *disclaimed responsibility* for it. The term "disclaimer" was introduced by Hewitt and Stokes (1975) and defined as "an interactional tactic employed by actors faced with upcoming events or acts which threaten to disrupt emergent meaning or discredit cathected situational identities" (Hewitt and Stokes 1975 p. 1). Schafer (1976) discusses the definition of "disclaimed action" and writes that such actions are a common part of our everyday existence and are often especially extreme in nature. Nonetheless, we feel compelled to confess that "my tongue slipped" or "I must have been out of my mind" (Schafer 1976 p.130).

The term "disclaimed action" captures well the essence of the passivity-activity ambiguity towards the man's behavior that was revealed in both the men's and women's narratives: the man's violent behavior was neither denied nor confirmed. The description of the violent action in terms of a "disclaimed action" removed the issue of the man's responsibility for what had happened from the agenda, and by that neutralized the incident.

In the account of my informants, I found two subtypes of neutralizations. The first type was when the act was disclaimed by means of a strong commitment to a good future. The act was then smoothed over with silence. When I pointed this out during the interviews, both men and women explained that they were not interested in "muckraking" or digging up the past, and that they were mature enough to consider it a closed chapter and to look forward.

The second type of neutralization was when the act was disclaimed through a rather intricate *redefinition* of the act by the offender or the victim, until the act had "dissolved", and the man was relieved from responsibility for it.

The accounts I classified as rejections were accounts in which the violent incident was strongly renounced. I found the rejection of the act strongly connected to a *rejection of either the man or the woman.* Four subtypes of rejections were found:

- The woman rejects the act and the *man*, expressing her fear and dissociating from him.
- The woman rejects the act and *herself*, due to her perception of herself as an inadequate person since she had been battered to such a degree.

– The man rejects the act and the *woman* on the basis of her behavior during the pre-history and violent incident.
– The man rejects the act and *himself*. This kind of rejection was found in two cases of the most severe violence.

Classifying by way of constructing

To continue my analytical work, I classified the accounts by their way of construction. I found them to be constructed in three different ways: (1) *jointly,* by the man and woman in cooperation; (2) *individually* constructed by the man; or (3) *individually* constructed by the woman. There was a tendency for my informants' accounts to follow one of the following patterns:

Neutralization of the violent act, as a **jointly constructed** account, encompassing hope for the good life.
Neutralization of the violent act, as a **jointly constructed** account, altering the meaning of the act.
Rejection of the violent act, as an **individually constructed** account, involving dissociation from the other or from oneself. (Table 7:1)

	Individually constructed	Jointly constructed
Rejection	Dissociation from other or oneself	----
Neutralization	----	Encompassing hope or altering of act

Table 7:1 Types of accounts of aftermath phase

The understanding of what had happened and the parties' conclusions as to what these incidents had meant for the marital and life projects was not self-evident for the woman and the man, nor easy to communicate. Due to my decision to follow my informants over a long period of time, it was possible for me as an outsider to study the different "modes of accounting". The process of understanding the vital modes is time-consuming however. So is the process of drawing conclusions about what determines whether it is possible or not to integrate a questionable marital act into the joint marital project.

Both means of trying to neutralize the violent action enhanced the possibility of integrating the act as a marital act. Of the seven couples who still lived together after two years, the majority described the violent act according to these patterns.

Ten couples separated over the course of the two years during which I had contact with them. Three couples established a "half-way" form of marriage, where the man was to remove himself to another dwelling during periods of discord. A majority of these couples had described the violent acts in terms of repudiation, in individually constructed accounts.

Neutralization of the violent act as a jointly constructed account, encompassing hope for the good life

Both kinds of accounts that neutralized the act were constructed jointly by the husband and wife. The man was generally the initiator of this joint enterprise, by dissociating himself from his own violent behavior. The initiation could take the form of pleading for forgiveness, showing remorse, or never-ending attempts at rehabilitation. Or as Hans A expressed it:

> The only way for me to show how much I love her after behaving so unforgivably is to buy her flowers and a ring. I love her so much. I keep telling her that. Everything is so good when we are together and everything is the way it should be - nice and cosy. (Hans A, individual interview)

Thus, a precondition for a joint construction of the account - which was the way of relating to the event that most certainly ensured its integration into the marriage - was the man's submission to the woman as the opening of the aftermath phase. Paradoxically enough, this position was easiest to maintain when the violent act was seen by the man as an "assault", due to its moral reprehensibility. It was evidently harder to adopt a corresponding position when the man viewed the act as a "fight". This distinction was even more troublesome since nineteen of the women assessed the acts in question as "assaults. Those men who called the acts "fights" thus were unable to agree with their wives in a joint appraisal.

As mentioned before, a "fight" is characterized by reciprocity, and the positions of perpetrator and victim are not clearly delimited in a pattern of dominance/subordination. The joint construction nevertheless demands that the man repudiates the act. In order to do this, he must refrain from criticizing the woman for her behavior during the fight, and he must adopt rationalizations for his wife's behavior. One of the men said his wife acted the way she did because she was unhappy and missed her family; another blamed his wife's behavior on her volatile temper. Finally, one of the men was of the opinion that his wife was dissatisfied with her life as a housewife:

What's wrong is that my wife has been shut in for 3–4 years, you know, yeah, about as long as we have lived here. She has stayed home with the kids and I have worked. Really hard. Often from nine in the morning to the middle of the night. She is really nice. But she has her outbursts just like I do. But I'm not trying to say this is her fault. She's been on her own for four years. Hardly ever seeing her husband. Finally, she attacks me too, to show 'I am a person'. (Ove T, individual interview)

This way of refraining from criticizing his wife for her behavior during the violent act but without really freeing her from responsibility for her actions does not mean that the husband here has altered his definition of the action into that of an "assault". By formulating his attention and concern about her as indulgence, he enhances the image of symmetry in their actions, and directs attention away from his dominance during the violent act. "She has her outbursts just like I do", says Ove T in the quotation above, and presents their "outbursts" as equivalents. In the wife's case, her "outburst" consisted of verbally expressed impudence, accompanied on one occasion by a flower vase being thrown at him. The husband's "outbursts" consisted of repeated incidents of her being beaten.

In this spirit of indulgence and symmetry, it is no longer difficult for the man to repudiate the violent act and to turn to the woman for a joint reconciliation after the violent act. At this moment, the woman has the power of self-determination:

Undoubtedly, I'm a little dumb. I think the whole time that it is going to get better, and when he also believes that it will get better and even promises that... but then I see that it doesn't get better. But the longer you are married, the more you get upset that you've stayed together so long – it feels like you've wasted time. /.../ I've thought about getting divorced many times. At this point I couldn't listen to his promises one more time... but I've had the children to consider. They have to have a father. My father died when I was very young. /.../ Then I thought I couldn't get along without him. So when he offers hope... lots of things make you want to hope. (Susanne O, individual interview)

The couples who agreed on jointly constructed accounts that encompassed a hope for the good life, all lived in accordant marriages. Their marriages were a very important precondition for success of their individual life projects, as these presupposed that they would live as husband/wife. A separation in this case would represent a substantial loss for the individual's life project. Furthermore, these couples had only limited or no experience of violence in their earlier lives. Finally, the violence that they had experienced had been of intermediate or minor seriousness.

This way of accounting for the violence focused on the *undesired consequences* for the joint marital project as well as for the individual projects:

> We really want to stay together, but a lot has to change if we do. These fights destroy so much. We have to learn to talk to each other and solve problems without fighting/.../ Our relationship is what you could call "a passionate relationship", with its ups and downs, but it always goes up after being down/.../ We have a good sex life... really good... I saw a TV program the other night. They said that good sexual relationships have a lot of playfulness. That's the way it is between me and Mats. We have everything we need – playfulness, tenderness. At those times, he really cares about me. (Annika R, individual interview)

> I don't like to fight. I've had too much fighting in my life. I have fought too much myself. So I try to avoid fighting with Annika. And that just ends up in a fight. I walk around steaming. If I've been drinking, then I can't keep it inside anymore. But then it usually turns out wrong... It's hard for me to sit down and explain things, to say what I want to say. After these fights, I am completely shattered. I don't want us to keep this up. (Mats R, joint interview)

By directing interest away from the act and towards its consequences, a husband and wife can come together with regard to their plans for a brighter future. They agree to leave the dark clouds behind them, and concentrate their energies on the time ahead. Nobody admits to anything in connection with the violent act, which is transformed into a disclaimed act through this process of "turning a blind eye".

Neutralizations of the violent act as a jointly constructed account, altering the meaning of the act:

> **I:** It got really serious the last time. You almost killed her.
> **IP:** Yeah, Ulla says so.
> **I:** What stopped it? What kept you from killing her?
> **IP:** You tell me; I'm hardly the best person you can ask since I don't remember anything. What she says happened is awful. She thought her last days had come. It's awful. I'll have to live with that for a long time. (Hans A, individual interview)

Like five other men, Hans had seriously battered his wife. He lived in a highly valued marital project. His individual project held a clearly subordinate position in relation to his marriage, or it could be said that it relied heavily on his marital project. He could not imagine living any other way than in a marriage with Ulla. For these reasons, he strongly repudiated the violent act. In the quotation above, he expresses this in terms of it being "awful" and that he does not "remember anything". He turns to Ulla and implores her not to leave him.

In the accounts which concern serious violence, it is the men who seek contact with the women during the aftermath phase. The women have sought medical attention for their injuries, and the men subjugate themselves to them. They plead arduously with the women and pressure them to become reconciled during the aftermath phase. In my opinion, it seems that these men desperately need their wives, not so much to save the marriage or even primarily to do so, but rather to save their own life projects. The strong rejection of both violence and themselves, pushes them into a state of crisis. Their wives are the only persons who can give them absolution after they have committed an "awful act" that they will have to "live with for a long time".

With regard to the violent acts of a less serious nature, there is always the possibility of overlooking the violent act and uniting for a better future. The steps that constitute such a "strategy of disregarding" were shown in the previous section: (1) A joint dissociation from marital violence. (2) The man's freeing the woman from responsibility for her behavior during the act, a "fight" in his eyes. (3) An invitation from him for her to enter into a joint enterprise of disregarding his use of violence and looking at a brighter future together. (4) Her acceptance of his offer.

An action that both designate as an "assault" and which has resulted in serious injuries to the woman cannot be overlooked in the same manner. From my informants' accounts, however, I have learned that it is possible to neutralize even such an action, regardless of whether or not the technique for doing so is extensive and complicated. In brief, since the act cannot be disregarded, this is a matter of altering the act so as to neutralize it. In this section, I shall try to give a step by step description of how this could be done.

What the couples agree to in regard to what happened in these cases could be formulated in one sentence, in a male version and in a female version:

I have beaten (assaulted) my wife.
I have been beaten (assaulted) by my husband.

Expressed in this manner, the meaning of the violent act constitutes a serious threat to the marital project as well as to the two individual life projects:

To accept the fact that you are a *battered woman* is almost impossible. I am so ashamed. For me, a battered woman is an unloved woman. I think that's why a woman won't go down to the grocery store with a big black eye. She doesn't want people to think, 'there goes the woman who has a man who beats her'. (Ulla A, individual interview)

I have hit her. I'd prefer not to think about it. But I am not a wife batterer. (Pablo J, individual interview)

In the narrative accounts of severe violence, I found that the action could be altered, until it no longer appeared to be threatening. What was needed can be described in terms of changing the sentences above. I identified three different ways in which this could be done:

Through changing the subject (the perpetrator) of the sentence.

Through changing the predicate (the act) of the sentence.

Through changing the object (the victim) of the sentence.

Changing of perpetrator: "Someone else beat me/my wife"
The most common way of changing the offender of the act, according to my informants' accounts, was to let alcohol take this role, and claim that alcohol had operated through the man and gotten him to commit the most horrible act:

He is two entirely different people. He's one when he is sober and another when he is drunk. When he doesn't drink, then he's himself. Then he's cheerful and pleasant, but also very shy. I think that's why he drinks. He plays the accordion. So when he is himself and is happy, he sings and plays the accordion. When he drinks, I don't recognize him any more. He gets restless and irritated. You don't need to say anything to him for him to get angry. And then he's capable of anything. (Ruth H, individual interview)

Under the influence of alcohol, it was no longer the man who did the beating. The alcohol had got the better of him.

One of the men alleged that it was his bodily constitution that was responsible for the beating:

You see, in our heads there is a place with two poles. There has to be a certain distance between them. When you get angry, you get close to one of the poles. In my head, the poles are too close together, so that when I get angry, they crash into each other. I can see on your face that you don't believe me, but this is true. A doctor himself told me this. I think it was caused by a motorcycle accident I was in. (Kjell I, joint interview)

I have already quoted Kjell in another context, in the discussion of methodology for combining and confronting my informants' stories. I then referred to his statements as to the *rhetoric of exculpation*. By altering the offense, Kjell could no longer be held fully responsible for his action.

Changing of act: "My husband/I slugged me/my wife"
It was striking how some of the women's accounts of the violent acts *diminished* over time. The act, labeled as assault in the first interview, could later become less and less significant. Or it could be redefined and described as some other type of act, such as a substitute for talking:

> It was always the case that I had an easier time to talk. During our arguments... I was always rather superior on that point. His words simply came to an end more quickly. Then he would start screaming and then start hitting. I think it was just his way of talking. I have read about this, that people express themselves in different ways, not only by talking. (Lisa Q, individual interview)

Changing of the victim: "My husband/I beat someone else"

> I can get really nasty about the least little thing. That's why he takes a go at me. For example, at the beginning of a fight, I can grab his newspaper. And so I always end up getting slapped. 'But hit me back', Hans says. 'No, I don't hit minors', I can throw back at him and then I know it's going to get hot. I can really be mean. When I get like that, yeah, I hate those sides of me as much as Hans does. (Ulla A, individual interview)

Ulla saw herself as cruel and a nag, at times. She tried to control these sides of her personality and hold them in check, but sometimes they got the better of her. She became belligerent and mean. Her perception was that her husband was beating these bad sides of her, sides that she condemned herself. When she assumed part of the blame, her image of her husband was preserved, and paradoxically even her self-image. She was not altogether an unloved woman according to this way of arguing and could retain a sense of being loved in spite of the violence ("it is the bitch he doesn't like, and I don't like her either"). Further, this process gave her a sense of control ("if I just could stop nagging, he would never beat me up again").

To transform the man's violent behavior into a disclaimed action

The main significance of the neutralizing process, in my opinion, is the effort to release the man from responsibility for his violent action. As early as in the accounts of the pre-history, a tendency to refrain from taking responsibility for his own behavior during the argument and to lay the blame on the other party, was observed. The argument that "*I am* doing this because my *partner* is doing that", was much more common than arguments like "*I am* doing this because *my* feelings have been hurt". Most men labeled the act "a fight", which implied restricting their responsibility to something they shared with their wives. On the other hand, the term "assault", when it was used unilaterally by the woman, indicated a description of the violent act which is aimed at forcing the man to understand the consequences of his actions for the woman and, therefore, not to repeat it. Finally, if both agreed to call the action an "assault", this indicated that both interpreted that which had happened as very serious. Both perceived the behavior as something that could not be allowed to continue, even if it was unclear as to what should be done to ensure that it would not recur. All three descriptions of the violent event were however capable of resulting in a total exculpation.

A total denial of an act that severely injured one of the parties of a marriage would bring immediate difficulties to that marriage. An active, responsible approach can also represent serious risk-taking. An entirely passive approach to the action, on the other hand, would imply extreme difficulties in seeking cooperation with the woman to neutralize his violent action. An account of the violent act as something for which he could not be held responsible eliminates such difficulties. By manipulating the act to the point where it becomes unclear as to who did what, the act was transformed into a "disclaimed action" (Schafer 1976). A "disclaimed action" is an action one neither takes direct responsibility for, nor remains entirely passive about.

What the narratives of the aftermath let us participate in, is the working up of a threat of separation and dissolution of the marriage, resulting from the men's conducting morally questionable marital actions. For it is not true that a battered woman never reflects upon leaving. On the contrary, she considers it constantly. Sometimes she leaves - but comes back. Sometimes she leaves for good. The battering man knows about this. This knowledge sometimes fills him with fear. If he will save his marriage, he must do something about it. As we here are dealing with a man experienced in the conduct of repeated violence, he knows that the odds for saving it are better if he succeeds in making the working up a joint enterprise for him and his wife.

The understanding that is desired, is in all humbleness an understanding that makes marriage possible. According to the narratives, the crucial point seems to be that *his credibility as husband is seriously called into question.* The means used for increasing credibility here, all seem to go in the direction of freeing him from responsibility: from his labeling of the act as a "fight", and thereby claiming shared responsibility with his wife, to his various ways of conducting the "rhetoric of exculpation", ending up in the disclaiming of the action.

The accounts revealed, that once the action was disclaimed, the man was freed from the charge of assault against his wife. He could then be permitted to continue as a marital partner. The violent incident no longer constituted a threat, either to the marriage or to his self-image. The joint marital project had been protected, and these couples could unite in their hope for a good future. But they paid a price for this.

At the same time that the man was freed from responsibility for his violent behavior, both partners lost access to their overall course of action of which the violent incident was a part. Neither of the partners had access to the powerful feelings of anger, despair, and hate that were linked to the violence. Therefore, it became impossible for them to integrate either the previous history, and/or the experiences of the violent incident into their individual projects, or to make them part of their joint experience.

Being acquitted from responsibility for the violent act means being freed from responsibility for a large part of one's individual life project. This way of neutralizing the act transforms the man into an irresponsible child, who is intermittently overwhelmed by aggression, intoxication, lack of words, and physical violence. The woman becomes the one who accepts all this, the one who absolves him. He is the irresponsible little person; she is the enduring bigger person. The significance of this kind of marital interplay will be discussed in the next chapter, as it constitutes an essential feature of the violent marriage, that is, a marriage with an extensive capacity to give refuge to violence.

Rejection of the violent act – individually constructed accounts revealing repudiation of oneself or the other

In an individually conducted interview, Fredrik P spontaneously commented on the violent incident:

> I have never regretted a single blow I gave her. For all the slugs she's gotten, she has deserved at least three times more. She is not at all weak or innocent. She can't hide behind the fact that she is a woman, and say or do anything. She acts like a man and is just as aggressive as a man. So she should just accept the fact that I treat her like this, that I slug her when she goes too far. (Fredrik P, individual interview)

Fredrik *admits the act* ("never regretted a single blow"), but *dismisses responsibility* for it. He describes the act as a fight, and he does not exonerate Nina in any way for her actions during the fight. On the contrary, she is held totally accountable. In his view, Fredrik should be seen as moderate and kind, since he has beaten her "three times less than she deserves".

This is not the kind of account that helps preserve a marriage. Altogether, twelve of the men accounted for the violent incident by rejecting the act and by repudiating the woman, even if not every man was as outspoken as Fredrik. He and another man, Rolf, both left their wives during the two-year study period. A majority of the other ten were involved in some kind of separation, or had distanced themselves from their wives to some degree.

A female equivalent to the above account could be illustrated by the following quotation from Irene:

> I was never hit at home, not as much as a slap from my parents. I think that that's why I react so strongly. The way I was brought up, you could get angry, but not hit./.../ You know, I have sometimes been able to calm him down. Maybe I just didn't want to this time/.../ When we are in the middle of a situation that turns into a fight, and I can't give in because I think I am right, that's when I don't want to calm him down. It would mean giving in, and that would be the same as admitting that I was wrong...so, it is not only to avoid losing the fight; it is also for my own self-respect. But it means that I am becoming more afraid; I don't know what he is liable to do. Whatever I do, it really shatters me/.../ All this has made me more and more unsure whether I have the strength to live with him. (Irene E, individual interview)

This statement was characterized by an orientation towards the woman's own life project. She believed that she could stop the man

from hitting her by assuming the subordinate position in a symmetrically escalating situation. But she also anticipated undesirable
consequences for her own individual project as an outcome of such
behavior. She said that "it is not good for my self-respect". She
forcefully rejected the act, and gradually dissociated herself from the
man.

In the two-year perspective, three of the five women who gave accounts of what happened similar to Irene E's left their marriages.
The two others established a "half-way" form of marriage, and arranged for an alternative place for their husbands to live during times
of disturbance. Both men initially rejected this solution, but the
women offered it as an unnegotiable condition for the continuance
of the marriage. All three women had come from what they considered "extremely gentle" families of origin, and had no expectations of violence related to family life. In these two types of accounts
of the violent act, the man's violent behavior was strongly
repudiated, and a dissociation (from the other party) by the woman
or by the man accompanied the rejection.

Two of the women dealt with the act by repudiating it, accompanied by a dissociation of themselves. This was the most tragic
course of action. Unlike the women who rejected their husbands for
the act, these women indicated that they wanted reconciliation, but
their request was rejected by their husbands. The two women had
both been subjected to severe violence in their family of origin. One
of these two women told me that she had been beaten so much that
she had already concluded that something must be wrong with her.
Depression and anxiety had tormented her throughout her life.
About her current situation, she said:

> I have been beaten so much in my life that I think there must be some-
> thing wrong with me./.../ It's hard living with myself nowadays...I hate
> it when it's messy and unfinished... My whole life is unfinished, but I
> don't do anything about it. I even admire Adam for putting up with me.
> (Viveka N, individual interview)

This way of accounting for the violent act revealed an abandonment
in relation to the marital project as well as the individual project. The
marriage continued on a "low-gear" basis, characterized by resignation, emotional distance, and anger.

By classifying the accounts according to content and the way of
constructing them, I ended up with three categories: two implying
neutralization of the violent act, and one its rejection. Each category
contained a small number of cases, every one providing me with con-

siderable information. I don't consider this categorization as complete and conclusive, however. I rather regard it as preliminary, and I will urge other researchers to continue. A larger sample could complete the picture perhaps by finding additional categories, by noting if any of the categories is more frequent than others, by adding new aspects to my findings.

The integration of violence in a long-term perspective

During the two years that I had contact with my informants, ten couples separated whereas seven continued to live together. Three couples perpetuated their close marital relation, but they periodically lived at different addresses.

Breaking Up

Eight of the women (Katrin C, Maria F, Marie G, Ruth H, Louise K, Kristina L , Lisa Q and Pirjo T) and two of the men (Rolf M and Fredrik P) claimed to have initiated their separation during the two-year study period. All of these women had declared their desire to get a divorce when they contacted the police or social authorities. Neither of the two men who had taken the initiative for a divorce meant that they had known this from the beginning; instead the decision had evolved with time. With regard to Gunilla and Rolf M, Gunilla had wanted to get a divorce from the beginning but changed her mind when Rolf took over the initiative for a divorce. Nina and Fredrik P initially wanted to continue as a couple, but Fredrik eventually changed his mind.

In the men's narratives, there was a direct link between the description of the violent incident as a "fight", in which the man viewed the woman's behavior as inexcusable, to a strong rejection of the incident and of her. During the course of the marriage, his image of her had undergone such alteration that she could no longer be his wife.

When I met Rolf M for the last time, he had been separated from Gunilla for almost one year, and had already begun a new relationship. He was quite preoccupied with that and with being as good a father to his children as possible. He talked of Gunilla as a thing of the past, and had I not known better, I would have thought that they had hardly known each other or had not meant much to each other.

Nor was the other man who separated, Fredrik, especially talkative when we met after his decision to separate. But he did show more contempt and anger towards Nina than Rolf did towards Gunilla. Gunilla simply no longer existed for Rolf.

The material I obtained from the men about what had led to their decision to divorce was extremely meagre. Once the decision was made, the marriage was treated as part of an uncomfortable past, not worth reflecting over. The material I obtained from the women as well was somewhat scanty. Therefore, what I present here is to be interpreted as a sketch of the process that lead women to break out of a violent marriage. Such a description would require further material and further precision.

In the women's accounts as well, a strong rejection of the act leads more often to separation than if the woman and the man together describe the act in a way that neutralizes it. The time factor though does play a role here. In the short run, it is the women who forcefully repudiate the act and who take the initiative for a divorce. Over the long run, this pattern is not as clear. Those women who are described by the police and social workers as "strong" women are over-represented here among those women who leave their marriages. Perhaps it is reasonable to interpret this so that "strong" in this context reflects the woman's ability to adhere to her *own* account of what she had experienced and not to change it by adopting the man's account as her own.

Over the long-term, it is feasible to view the violent act as a threat to the woman's life project "from two directions". Her life project is threatened due to the destructive effect the violence has on it – but also from the effect on her joint marital project. The later threat may be just as strong as the first for those women who highly value their marital project and who consider it a prerequisite for a successful life project.

In the accounts from women who leave their marriages, two themes emerge: the lost hope for a brighter future for the marital project and a longing to lend the life project a new direction. The three voices below reflect these themes:

> It's not that I've given up hope for our marriage. It's more that I've given up hope that it's going to be good. I am really tempted to leave this thing with Carl-Magnus, the whole thing. Out into the world, out into reality, and leave this confining, chained life that I'm sinking into. But out, in my own apartment, to meet people, do what I want, have my own friends, be left in peace in the evenings. That's what I want. To start all over and see what life outside of this place is all about. (Kristina L, individual interview)

I thought it was so bloody warped. He drank up all our food money and everything and then lied straight to my face: 'I didn't do this' and 'I didn't do that'. He didn't take any responsibility. It was me who had to fix everything. I am so angry and disappointed in him and in the hospital [Erik had been admitted for treatment for his alcoholism, author's note]. He can do just about anything, and they'll still admit him when he wants to come back. But I am also a person. I want to be taken into account. They can't walk all over me. (Marie G, individual interview)

You think all the time that it's going to get better, and he promises that too. But then you see that it doesn't get better. But you continue anyway. I'm probably a little stupid too. You get so sad about having stayed together so long. It feels like you've completely wasted your time. But now it's like I have lost all hope that anything will ever be different. It is so tragic. (Ruth H, individual interview)

These women express strong feelings of *grief* and *anger*. In some of the women's accounts, the feeling of hate dominates:

Now there's just this hate. In fact, I feel such disgust, that if I could choose, I would never see him again. Sometimes I want revenge so badly, that if he turned up here... yeah, I would cut his dick off, 'coz he doesn't deserve to have one. Or I'd put him up against the wall and shoot him. I can get so mad that I become afraid of myself. I would like to kill Ismeth. I don't intend on being afraid anymore. (Lisa Q, individual interview)

Hope as well as sorrow that one's hopes have not been fulfilled, as expressed by Ruth and in part Kristina, and the hate that Lisa and in part Marie express, derive from different sources of energy: hope from love and life and the dream of togetherness, and hate from the wish for destruction and death. Both are sustained though by the perpetually unfulfilled desire for respect from the other partner. These feelings are similar in another way as well: both bind. Hope binds the hopeful person to that person her hope is about. Hate binds the hater to the hated person as if to a loved one.

Perhaps in contrast to common conceptions, I do not view hate as a divider, nor solely as the force of individuation, the opposite of love, or the servant of separation. On the contrary, hate wants to knock the object of hate down to the hater's level, in order for them to meet there as peers, as hope wants to lift the object of hope to an encounter on the hopeful one's level.

In other words, when a woman adopts an attitude of hope or hate, she finds her life project in the shadow of her husband's. Her life is dependent on what he does. In the position of hoper or hater, she makes herself the victim of his rampages. When the woman becomes a victim, I believe that she in some sense always forgets who she is, from where she came, and to where she is going. She sacrifices her life project for the marital project.

A very tragic example of this is Gunilla. She cannot stop thinking about how disgusting Rolf is, about how much he has hurt her, and she feels he is still persecuting her. She sees his car outside her office, so she does not dare go to work anymore. She sits at home with the curtains drawn. She organizes her life according to the basic notion that a man like Rolf will never cause her anything but pain. In reality, he is already living with another woman and Gunilla is "forgotten". Gunilla has developed increasingly paranoid tendencies and was admitted to a mental hospital, whereupon Rolf gained custody of their children.

If hope or hate are not both abandoned, the women's own life project will remain invisible. From what I have been able to read from the women's accounts about their separations, the road there is lined with sorrow and the resignation that the man will never change and will "remain as loathsome as ever". A separation leads to a feeling of emptiness and sorrow, but also opens up new possibilities. My encounter with the six women who separated from their husbands has led to a renewed respect for the emotional difficulties that a woman faces when undergoing a separation. If we add practical and economic difficulties to this, we undoubtedly have part of the explanation why women – and men – remain in marriages that are catastrophic for their life projects.

"Half-way marriages"

The following quotations were taken from an interview with Vladimir E:

> **IP:** Yeah, we are going to remain a couple but we'll move apart.
> **I:** Really?
> **IP:** This is our plan anyway. We'll see. If it becomes good again, maybe we'll live together for real.
> **I:** But for now, you will each have your own apartment...
> **IP:** We will keep contact with each other. That's our plan. Because we have children together. You have to think about that too.
> **I:** How has this happened... what led to your moving apart?
> **IP:** Well [some laughter], I like to party sometimes, and Irene doesn't like to. It's her that's decided this. That if I go partying, I'm not to come home. I have to stay at my own apartment. So I have had to find a little one-room apartment in the area.

I: So, this is an area you disagree about. But now you solve it by each of you having your own home. So you avoid getting all upset about this.

IP: Exactly. Then we'll see what happens. Maybe we'll like living alone. It's tiresome to move back and forth all the time. But it is Irene who decided. I said I would start behaving better, but it didn't help.

I: So it was Irene who decided....

IP: .... and I who obey her commands [laughs]!

In the three couples (Irene and Vladimir E, Viveka and Adam N, Lena and Birger S) who eventually arranged what I call "half-way marriages", all of the women have (like Irene in the quotation above) been the ones to push through these changes. The basic idea seems to be the same: the woman has failed in getting the man to change himself within the framework of their marriage, so she makes conditions for the continuation of their marriage. Two of these women were initially categorized as "strong" women, who forcefully repudiated the violent act. One of the women is in the opposite category. Her "half-way marriage" was the result of weariness and a general sense of futility rather than of decisiveness and the drawing of clear boundaries.

Continued co-residence

As was the case for the couples who separated, it is possible to discern early on in the aftermath the tendency towards a decision to stay. Among these seven who continued to live together, there was a distinct tendency to neutralize the violent act and to publicize what had happened as little as possible:

> You don't talk about this kind of thing. A couple of people I've talked to know about it... They know he's going to be sentenced and they think it's good. It's no secret to them, they are my only girlfriends. But I would never have told them if I hadn't intended to get a divorce. Then I wouldn't have wanted anything to come out. /.../ They think that I'm totally crazy to take him back. I even got flowers from a friend of mine when I told her I was going to take out a divorce. Now she is really upset: 'You can't be so dumb as to take him back. We still want to have you as a friend.' But they really know very little about our feelings for each other. About how we sit and talk with each other. That we in fact have it good together. (Ulla A, individual interview)

The fact that knowledge about the violent act is not spread outside of the family facilitates the neutralization and integration of the event within the marital project. The couple is then able to develop its own framework for interpretation, without being disturbed by competing interpretative frameworks.

All twenty informant couples had in some way gone public with the violence in their marriage, either *directly* by relating what had happened to the social authorities or to the police, or *indirectly* by the women being forced to seek medical treatment. For those couples who continue as couples, having made the violence public is a factor that needs to be dealt with. At this point, the couple needs to consider the surrounding world's interpretation of the violent act and its conclusions as to the consequences of the violence for the marriage. "The surrounding world", whether it be girl friends, health workers, or social workers, are described in the women's narratives as persons who are convinced that the battered women ought to leave their violent husbands:

> They were very adamant about me getting a divorce while I was still in the hospital. So I did. Then I took the papers back. It was quite embarrassing, because then I couldn't talk about what happened. (Ulla A, joint interview)

The accounts given by those informants who continued to live together reveal two patterns for dealing with the surrounding world's expectations for change in their marriages. One approach was isolation from the outside world. One of the couples (Pia and Kjell I) rented a house out in the country and moved there with their children. Another couple (Angela and Pablo J) went in the same direction in a manner that greatly distressed me.

At our final meeting – a result itself of a great deal of persuasion on my part – Angela was pale and thin, and Pablo looked tense and was dismissively friendly. Pablo had been released after having served a prison sentence for aggravated assault. At the beginning of Pablo's prison sentence, Angela was determined to follow through on the divorce she had filed for in the hospital. When she started visiting Pablo in prison, she began changing her mind. But what ultimately got her to change her mind were her two children, seven and nine years old. They begged and pleaded for her to allow their father to come home again. "Come and I'll show you that we are a family again", Angela says to me and takes me into the bedroom. There lay a baby girl, only a few months old, sleeping in her crib. "She is the proof of our love", says Angela. She explained to me that now they had proven to the world that the past was forgotten, they did not want to discuss the past anymore, neither with me nor anyone else. Our contact was thus terminated.

The second of the two approaches for dealing with the surrounding world's expectations did not involve a reinforcement of old interactional patterns, but rather an attempt at change. This endeavor for change was expressed in some of the men's accounts (Hans A; Mats R). These men described a powerful urge to find new ways of dealing with the situations that had normally led to fights. The following dialogue takes place between Mats (M) and Annika (A), where he tries to explain during our final meeting how he had tried to change his style and "not get all heated up" all the time:

M: Something happened last Friday. It wasn't much, but it meant a lot to me. Annika wanted us to go out dancing at a place nearby. She sounded very determined. I didn't want to go. We had been there before and then it was filled with a bunch of brutes that kept getting into fights.
A: But you didn't say that. You just said you didn't want to go, not why you didn't.
M: No, you're right. When she takes that determined tone, I try not to start arguing with her. But that never works. So we went to the dance place. I could tell immediately that there was going to be trouble that night. People were pretty drunk even though it was early. So then I got mad at Annika for bringing me there. I wasn't entirely sober either. The situation was ripe for a huge fight. Then I remembered what we had talked about when you were here and I decided I didn't want to fight. *I did not want to fight again.* So I just left. I went home and was cooking some food when Annika came in. She was really surprised. She didn't say anything at first, but then asked me how I was. And for the first time, I got to say everything I wanted to say [laughs].
A: I would never have known that you didn't want to go there because you were afraid there'd be fights. I thought you didn't want to go there mostly 'coz I did want to. Next time, you can tell me why. It's too much work to drag everything out of you all the time. (Mats and Annika R in a joint interview)

In the quotation below, Hans A (H), expresses similar thoughts to the interviewer. This quotation, from the final interview with Hans and Ulla, will end this chapter on the short-term and long-term aftermath of the violent act. In the following chapter on "the violent marriage", I will return to the discussion of the possibilities for change within a marital project that has over many years integrated the man's violence against the woman, but where the parties involved nevertheless want to stay married and continue living together.

H: I have wondered a lot about how to avoid all this in the future since I have such a hot temper.
I: Do you have any suggestions?

H: To never really get started. Instead of protesting, just leave. Or start talking about something else. Most important is not to talk about anything that can lead to a fight except when I'm sober/.../ I used to have this really stupid habit before. I would start drinking to calm myself down after Ulla and I started to fight. It was crazy. It only resulted in me getting really angry. I've stopped doing that.

I: I think you are the type that likes to talk to someone when you get upset.

H: That's bloody right. That's why I talked the thing to death when Ulla and I fought. The more angry and sad I got, the more I kept talking in this reasonably pleasant way. Last time we fought, I left and went to a friend's and drank a beer. Most guys know how women are! [laughs]. [Turns toward Ulla:] No, honey, you know I don't think you're a bitch, it's just something guys say! (Hans and Ulla A in a joint interview)

A note on the integration of violence into a marriage

One of the most commonly asked questions in discussions about woman battering is, "Why does a woman stay with a man who repeatedly beats her?" The question contains an undertone of skepticism about the woman's behavior: "Can a woman who lives with a violent man be entirely normal?" Strangely enough, the corresponding question about the man's behavior is not usually asked. This kind of questioning, irrespective of whether the question has been directed towards a woman or a man, leads one's thoughts to the parties' *personalities*. Furthermore, the skeptical undertone of these questions seems to presuppose a given answer: "These are in all likelihood people who suffer from an impaired ability to reach reasonable decisions about their own lives."

The conversations with my informants have taught me that this way of asking questions is too restrictive, too narrow, if we are to understand how it is possible to continue a marriage in spite of repeated violence against the woman. In the aftermath of the violent act, the involved parties weigh what the violent act has meant for them and their marriage. This process is certainly influenced by their personalities, but becomes difficult to understand if the entire phenomenon is solely seen in an individual psychological perspective.

People's appraisal of what occurs in their own marriages is largely related to the images they have about what a marriage should entail and what it should offer the individual woman and man. People value the significance of the marital project differently. For many people, a marriage is a necessary precondition for life, a fact that ensures the joint project a strong position in these people's lives. For other people, the joint marital project is of less importance for their individual projects. Taken together, these different approaches are significant for the way in which people value the violent incidents that occur in their marriages.

My informants reached different and completely divergent conclusions about the meaning of the violent action. I have found the action strongly repudiated by the battering man or the battered woman, a repudiation that was accompanied by an equally strong rejection of the other spouse. I have found the violent action neutralized by the battering man and the battered woman in a joint enterprise.

Over a two-year perspective, those couples who neutralized the violence had the greatest chance of surviving as a couple. Not surprisingly, I have also found a correlation between the significance that my informants attach to their marriages and the conclusions that they reach during the aftermath of the violent act. Those couples where the marriage was of great importance to both parties tend to join forces and neutralize the violent act, whereas the men and women who contend that their marriage was not of great significance for their lives tend to repudiate both the action and the other party forcefully.

Compared to the significance of the marital project and the life projects for the process of attaching meaning to the man's violent behavior, the *degree of seriousness* of the violent incident was found to be of little consequence. I was surprised to learn that a mild slap could be repudiated as strongly as a sharp blow, and that an act of severe battering could be neutralized in the same way as a shove. In this context, the battered woman's experience of violence in her family of origin was seen as an important factor.

There was no evidence in my study of a systematic difference between couples with "immigrant backgrounds" and other couples with regard to the significance of the violent act for the marriage.

The battered woman's earlier experiences of violence were thus of importance, but not as factors leading to an increased risk for her to be battered. A woman can be the victim of her husband's violent behavior without any previous experience of family violence, and a man can commit a violent act without having witnessed, or having been subjected to, male violent behavior in his family of origin. But earlier experiences of family violence do play an important role in the aftermath of the violent outburst, in the process of making sense of and reaching conclusions about what had happened. The earlier victimized women were more likely to confront their husband's behavior by assuming a subordinate position, and they tended to accept their husbands' invitations to join forces in the neutralization of the man's violent behavior. On the other hand, those women who had no experience of the direct use of physical violence in the family context, tended to dissociate themselves sharply from both the violent act and the perpetrator.

In this context, it is worth noting that both the narrative accounts where the violent incident was powerfully repudiated and the neutralizing accounts contained the same distinct dissociation from the man's use of violence. The rejecting accounts explicitly expressed this, and the neutralizing accounts indirectly expressed this through the effort that went into neutralizing the action.

A reformulation of the questions of why the woman or the man stays, in spite of violent incidents, encompassing those aspects of central importance for the parties' own determinations in the aftermath of the violent incident, would be: *"What compels her to continue her efforts to get him to stop using violence, despite the fact that the repetition of the violence is a reflection of her continual failure?"* A corresponding question for the man would be: *"If he in fact wants the relationship to continue, why does he time after time commit questionable acts that in and of themselves increase the risk that the relationship will be ended?"*

Reformulated in this way, the questions presuppose that the issue of staying or leaving the marriage is related to the *possibility of integrating the violent acts into the marriage as marital acts.* I here use the word "integrating" to describe the process of maintaining the marital relationship, not the acceptance of the violence. Merely the ability to continue in a relationship where such violent situations have and do occur is what is meant here.

The first point worth noting here is that over a two-year period, half of my informants' marriages ended in divorce, eight at the initiative of the women and two at the men's. The majority of the women who took the initiative in the divorce had declared at the start of the study period that they were contemplating divorce. In contrast, the men reached this decision during the course of the study. Another three couples continued to live together, but at two addresses so that the man could withdraw "in times of trouble". Seven couples continued living together as usual.

An integration of the violent incident always implies that the woman's individual life project is pushed into the background in favor of the joint marital project. The driving force for this may be that the marital project is highly valued – but it may also be that she and others assign such a low priority to her life project. This tendency is strengthened during the course of the integration process. The import for a battered woman to enter into a joint enterprise aimed at neutralizing the violent act is a gradual devaluation of her own life project. On this point, my female informants displayed similar patterns to those found in other research studies on battered women around the world (Dobash and Dobash 1979; Walker 1979; Araldsen and Clasen 1983; Christensen 1984).

I had categorized six of the seven women who continued to live with their husbands as "fragile" in the original classification of informants. During the study period, it was revealed that at least three of these women had gradually become more "fragile" during the course of their marriages. Their weakness should thus be viewed as a consequence of their marital life, and not vice versa. Prior to getting married, one of the "fragile" women, Sonja B, managed a store in a large franchise chain in her hometown. Now she is a steady customer at her local health center where she is treated for severe anxiety problems. Fathima D, likewise described as "fragile", was a teacher in her country of origin and now suffers from anxiety attacks, thinks she is going to die, and is convinced that she is seriously ill.

Paradoxically, the same process of integration that leads to a devaluation of one's own life may also add something to it. Since the integration process means that the spouses start working together towards a neutralization of the violent act, they may also experience an intense feeling that the marital project is gaining something: togetherness and communality.

For the man, the circumstances are somewhat more complex than for the woman. In one sense, his life project gains something from his violent behavior, namely, the experience of power and of total control and dominance over the woman he lives with. With the integration of the violent act into the marriage, he receives reassurance that such an act does not lead to the collapse of the marriage. On the contrary, it leads to community and togetherness. But the integration of the violent act has another meaning for the man, which is related to the fact that he committed an act not only questionable as a marital act but also questionable from the perspective of his own life project.

It is my conclusion that by committing this questionable act against their wives and yet dissociating themselves from the act – which is necessary for the neutralization of the event, and thus its integration – the men continue in a state of crisis. Their wives are the only ones who can absolve them for such "awful" acts. Their wives are the ones who will cooperate with them in manipulating the act to the point where it becomes unclear as to who did what, to the point where the act was transformed into a disclaimed act. In other words, to the point where the man is freed from all responsibility for his action.

No one else but the wife can do that for the man. Other male acquaintances may support the man in his rejection strategies – and in the notion of the impossibility of women and so on – but they cannot join with him in a neutralization strategy to preserve the marriage.

I believe that this dependence is fundamental for the man. Undoubtedly, faulty conclusions are reached if an attempt is made to interpret the battering man who after a separation continues to threaten and abuse the woman in his desire to reunite with her. It is not necessarily the case that he wants to win her back. But it is her power to grant absolution and to restore his self-esteem and value that he needs. The ultimate evidence of this is her willingness to continue in the marriage.

His behavior also leads to a devaluation of his own life project in another sense. In order to plead with his wife for her cooperation in neutralizing his actions – even for the sake of his life project – he is compelled to refrain from criticizing his wife for her behavior during the pre-history of the violent incident. This means that regardless of how much he feels she has hurt him, he cannot tell her this.

These conclusions may be partial answers to the question of why a man and a woman remain in a marriage in which violent episodes repeatedly occur.

The aftermath – a summary

The last phase of the violent event is characterized by a dissociation/integration process where the man and the woman, separately and jointly, evolve an understanding of what had happened.

In the aftermath of the violent incident, the pattern of dominance and subordination reveals its superior position as creator of the social organization of my informants' marriages. Thus, to improve the chances for the survival of the marriage, the man voluntarily places himself in the subordinate position as a necessity for the commencement of the aftermath.

Two principal patterns can be discerned in my informants' accounts. One of these basic patterns involves the neutralization of the violent event, where the man and the woman jointly construct a narrative account of what had happened. This type of account may encompass either a hope for the good life or an alteration of the act. Both types of neutralizing accounts imply great possibilities for the integration of the action into the marriage.

The second principal pattern for the development of such an understanding involves a rejection of the violent act. A rejection of the act proved to be strongly related to a rejection of either the man or the woman, according to one of the following combinations:

– *her* rejection of the act and the man, expressing her fear and dissociation from him;
– *her* rejection of the act and herself, due to her conception of herself as an inadequate person after so much battering;
– *his* rejection of the act and the woman, on the basis of her behavior during the pre-history and violent incident;
– *his* rejection of the act and himself, since he had committed such a severe act of violence.

The concrete results of this dissociation/integration process can be summarized under three headings: divorce, continued living together, or "half-way-marriage", that is cohabitation but with access to separate dwellings.

8

The Violent Marriage

Introduction

In this study, I have chosen to analyze "woman battering" as a social phenomenon that has arisen through the exercise of some types of violent actions (a man's) in a certain social context (a marriage) against a particular person (the woman/wife), and that has been described and characterized through a process of historical and social definition. This process of social definition must basically be understood as a *web of voices* which from different directions try to define, delimit, describe, and explain "woman battering". These voices may emanate from sociology, psychology, or feminism, and they are heterogeneous in the sense that they cannot be merged into a single definition of "woman battering". Instead, the distinct voices must be analyzed in the light of their own premises.

With the operation of this process, it has become possible for both women and men to begin defining their own and others' actions in terms of this social definition. Women and men will discuss the "woman battering" they have been subjected to (women) or that they want to be exculpated from responsibility for (the men). In this manner, men's violence against women within marriage has become a possible field of study within the social sciences.

To avoid becoming entrapped within a more or less normative definition of "woman battering", I have chosen to study not only the course of the violent incident, but also the involved parties' means for defining this incident and their possible responsibility for it.

It is the emergence of women from a solitary existence as victims that generates the disclosure of men's violent actions towards women. This study can be described as a response to this stepping forward of battered women, as well as its condition. My goal with the study has been to understand the socio-psychological process that "woman battering" entails for the two involved parties separately (and in part also for the children) and jointly, and in part to understand how the police and social authorities define what had happened.

The study group consisted of cases that were defined over the course of one year by the police and social authorities in a Stockholm suburb as "woman battering". Altogether, this group included 141 cases. Some basic data on the battering files were collected from this group, where the violence mainly ranged from serious to medium-serious, where 49% of the men and 33% of the women were under the influence of alcohol, and where the woman's injuries were more serious if she and/or the man were intoxicated at the time of battering.

From among the 141 couples, I selected a smaller group for studying the process of marital woman battering. After attempts to achieve a balanced sample of couples with regard to the degree of seriousness of the violence, personal characteristics of the woman, and socio-economic status, my sample consisted of twenty couples. I – and in some cases a male colleague – interviewed these couples separately and together over a period of two years.

This interview material constituted the basic material for my description of the cyclical process of marital violence. My primary goal has been to contribute to the identification of the *rules and conventions* which determine the parties' behavior during the violent incident as revealed in the parties' descriptions, explanations, and justifications for the marital violent act.

What I found to be central for the development of a violent marriage are the special means by which couples *live their marital lives*, in the manner in which they make sense of the marital acts within their marriage, and how they *deal with the fundamental social rule* about male violent behavior as a marital action. By "violent marriage" is meant a marriage where violent incidents occur and are integrated as marital acts, a marriage with extensive capacity to give refuge to violence.

Living marital life

When two individuals enter into a marriage with each other, their form of life is radically transformed towards one of marital life. By marrying each other, the woman and man are transformed into something whose psychological import could be described in terms of the two individuals defining themselves in relation to the other person. One cannot be a spouse without there being another spouse. Your identity as a married woman or a married man depends on the other.

Being a marital spouse, however, is not something that can be imputed to a person, something that is applied passively, for example,

by genetic or historical forces. It is something that the involved parties determine and develop together. In this perspective, the marriage
is something that is *socially constructed*, something that is actively
created with both parties serving as agents. I have described the
modes by which the couples designed their social organization of
marital life in terms of the partners forming a *joint marital project*.

To describe a marriage in terms of a project necessitates the introduction of the dimension of time. This means that a marriage is
not only viewed in terms of the given or current situation, but more
accurately *in light of its future*. The project is the expression of the
marriage's goals and contents in constant fluctuation, in which the
marital scene and the acts performed thereon continually influence
each other. To participate in this cooperative project, from the plat-
form of the individuals' given preconditions, means that the actors
are neither the helpless victims of a predestined fate nor the creators
of an ultimate perfect future.

By introducing the dimension of time as a fundamental factor in
the organization of marital life, I span a bridge between the
theoretical perspective I have evolved for understanding what it is
that characterizes marital life and the methodological approach I
have used to study violence as a marital act. A person's account of
what has happened in her or his life contains both a retrospective and
a prospective dimension. The stories or the narratives of our lives not
only precede us through our parents' and ancestors' histories – in
which we are more or less enmeshed – but also face to an equal degree
ahead. By means of our ability to imagine a possible future, the narrative will determine our manner of approaching our dreams, our
desires, and our fate.

To give form to a successful joint project, the parties must be
capable of dealing with – and of developing – the underlying rules
for the marital life style that have evolved in our society. Here I do
not mean rules in the sense of regulations about how a husband and
a wife "are", but rather the rules that generate husbands and wives
from men and women. In the sense that I here use the concept of
"rule", it is something that "makes" a married couple and in this
way gives the marriage form.

Up to this point, I have discussed what could be said to apply
generally to marital life. That which characterizes those marriages I
have studied and distinguishes them from marriages in general is that
they include *repeated violent actions* by the man against the woman.
These violent incidents are of a cyclical nature and consist of three
separated phases that are repeated over many years. In principle, this
cycle is broken temporarily by intervention from external agents

(such as the police or social authorities) or more permanently if the woman – and in some cases the man – leaves the marriage.

The first phase of the violent cycle consists of the pre-history of the violent incident and is described as a verbal aggressive act, or as a desire for revenge, or as a desire to compel the wife to remain in the marriage in the case of imminent divorce. The second phase consists of the violent incident, and the last phase of the process of dissociation/integration that constitutes the aftermath of the violent incident.

Rules of woman battering in a Swedish cultural context

I began this study with the assumption that the "rule" which constitutes a marriage in a Swedish cultural context and which influences how men and women deal with violent incidents in all probability could be summarized by the following statement: Violence is a morally questionable marital act. As a result of what I have learned from this study, I would propose changing the rule somewhat to make it more forceful and distinct:

> Woman battering within a marriage is not an acceptable act. It is not an act a woman within the Swedish cultural context should expect as a consequence of her love for a man.

My material does not support the belief that the time-worn notion "you beat the one you love" enjoys a strong foothold in the context of contemporary Swedish marital life, or the approach of Moa Martinsson's fictional characters, "Bernard" and his next door neighbor, as quoted in the introduction, that "when your woman starts acting devilishly, just hit her".

I have had the opportunity to observe the above formulated rule in operation principally in the narratives about the aftermath phase. A violation of this rule triggers off a threat of separation. In this perspective, the aftermath phase could be viewed as one extensive attempt to avoid that threat. As the couples account for the violent act by neutralizing it, they not only reveal their idea of this rule, but also of how they want to appear in the eyes of others. "You get shamed in front of others; you imagine that they think that your husband doesn't love you" (Ulla A, individual interview). There are only two ways for a woman to resolve this dilemma: by dissociating herself from the violent act and her husband, or by manipulating the action so that the man is exculpated from responsibility for it.

The social order of a violent marriage

In the chapter on the pre-history of the violent act, I made an initial remark about the social order prevailing in the marital projects of my informants. I concluded that as the spouses fought verbally, they also created basic forms of social order. "The one-up-manship and attempts to put the other down pattern" of interaction was strictly adhered to during the verbal fights. Asked about the frequency of these fights, nine couples admitted to fighting "often" or "always", and eleven "not so often" or "often". From among the couples with a high frequency of verbal fights, two claim that their fights almost always turn into more serious fights, that is, violent encounters. The remaining seven who fight often say that their fights do not always develop into something serious. The figures for the couples with a low frequency of verbal fights are the reverse: Eight of those couples maintain that their fights almost always develop into serious arguments, whereas three couples claim that this does not occur.

I concluded that the role of the pre-history was constitutive in producing a hierarchical organization within the marital projects, following *a basic pattern of dominance and subordination*. The prominent feature of the social process during the verbal fight was composed of the endeavor to bring the status of the other person into question, and to demote her or him to a lower ranking. The principal means for accomplishing this was the *mutual communication of worthlessness*. Well adapted to this purpose was the exploitation of the other's weaknesses, recounting embarrassing events of the past, or listing the bad traits of the other party. Due to the fact that the pre-history of the violence turns into the violent phase itself, the hierarchical pattern becomes transfixed in a single image: the man in the dominant position and the woman in the subordinate position.

In brief, this pattern of male dominance and female subordination, as it is expressed during the phase I have described as the violent incident, has been the concern of feminist researchers and of the women's movement. In spite of the similarity between their conclusions and mine, I can identify some significant differences. In my opinion, a husband's use of violence towards his wife, and the way she reacts to it produces social order, and as well reflects an already existing social order in the surrounding society.

In the view of some feminist researchers, the use of physical violence against women in their position as wives is not the only means by which they are controlled and oppressed. Nevertheless, it is one of the most brutal and explicit expressions of patriarchal domination. According to this view, the dominance a husband practices over his wife is something *externally imputed to him*. He and his wife could jointly be considered victims of patriarchy, even if he is generally believed to be the one deriving an advantage from this mode of victimization. According to the linguistic usage I have adopted (see further Schafer 1976), I will refer to this way of accounting for a man's use of violence towards his wife as a way of *disclaiming* his action. By handling the ambiguity between passivity and activity of human action in this manner, the action of the individual man becomes masked.

During the violent incident, the hierarchical organization within the marriage assumes a more definite shape. By the use of violence, the man usurps power over the woman. "Power over" refers to domination and control. "Power over" generally carries destructive consequences because of its self-serving and restricting nature. True for the use of power over another human being in general, it is even more dramatically true for a battered wife.

When the man's dominance is expressed by means of violence in this rigid and illegitimate manner, this affects both the woman's individual life project and joint marital project. Her subordination becomes visible by means of her inability to protect herself and by means of her failed attempts to form the marriage in the way she so desires. In the women's accounts, this inability was described sometimes as failed attempts to decrease the man's relative dominance by adopting a defensive position and submitting to an even greater degree. Or it was described in terms of an increasing reluctance, which is due to the woman's way of protecting herself causing encroachment in her own individual life and her "crawling her way to nonrecognition".

This use of illegitimate means in order to maintain a dominant position thus results in a shift of positions during the aftermath phase. Retaining the rigid pattern of dominance/subordination, the positions are shifted so that the man lands in the inferior position. He is the one who has committed an unacceptable act, and she has been the object of this act and endured it. In order to "save" his marriage, the man has to act in accordance with the prevailing rules operating within the context of a Swedish marriage, and dissociate himself from the violent act, and then implore his wife for a joint reconciliation. This means that he temporarily holds a subordinate position, whereas her relative influence is enhanced. However, her enhanced relative influence is limited to the issue of whether she will accept his remorse or not, and whether she will accept his offer for joint action or not.

Thus, what happens in the aftermath of the violent act is not renegotiations about how a wife and a husband basically deal with the issue of power in the marriage. *The rigid pattern of dominance and subordination is not affected at any point during any of the phases of the violent act.* What is affected is the allocation of positions within the established pattern.

The temporary and limited dominance given to women whose husbands are desperate and repentant during the aftermath of the violent act, provides these women with relatively more power to influence the form of their marital life. In the moment that the husband subordinates himself to his wife and pleads with her to join efforts with him, she has the power to determine whether the marriage will continue or not.

If she uses her power to say yes, the effect of this for the future marriage is ambiguous. As the person who does the forgiving and who endures, she is relatively strong; but as the person who is battered and who wishes to continue living with her batterer, she is relatively weak. In contrast, the man has proven that he has the strength to dominate her totally, but by means that are morally reprehensible.

If there were cause to use an expression like *the violent marriage*, I think it could be used for labeling the above described social order. This kind of marital project is primarily characterized by rigid and paradoxical rules for the distribution of power. That which makes the man strong, dangerous, and dominant in this type of marriage, also makes him small, helpless, and dependent on his wife. That which makes the woman weak, helpless, and dependent is also that which makes her strong in the sense of perseverance and patience. In addition, this kind of marital project generates an interaction neutralizing the violent act, by disclaiming the man's reponsibility for it.

Possibilities for change

The socio-psychological interior that I have gained insight into through my informants' narratives is quiet dismal. Two individuals who hope for a life together which is better than their separate lives, enter into marriage and interplay within a closed space according to rules that exclusively allow a rigid social order of dominance and subordination. When the man usurps the dominant position by illegitimate means, he further increases the couple's isolation. Now they have something to hide. Nor is the probability especially high that the "surroundings" will demand admittance. According to the

Swedish view of marriage, marital life is strictly private. The most revolutionary action in the direction of change is here undertaken by the woman, as she decides to step forward and prepares herself to talk.

Over a two-year period, ten couples found a way out. A study which examines what follows such a separation over the long run is an important research task.

After two years, two of the still-married men describe a change in their manner of dealing with a situation which formerly could have constituted a prelude to a violent act. They have decided they do not want to use violence. By taking responsibility for their actions, they construct a sphere of action which they use to break their usual behavior patterns. They refrain from taking control over the situation and simply distance themselves from it.

I would like to say three things to those outsiders who approach such couples for the purpose of facilitating change – such as social workers or psychotherapists:

> – Learn to understand the couple's own text to see what is expressed and what is not expressed. Be attentive to your own role in this context; in other words, be attentive to what going public means for the parties.
>
> – Confront the logical frame of the accounts.
>
> – Assist the two parties in constructing a new story.

During such endeavors, one always first encounters the special "rhetoric of exculpation" described above. Here there is a need to listen carefully to what the woman and the man have to say, in order to identify defensiveness and rationalization. There is a need also to examine what the two parties say, in order to deconstruct minimizing, externalizing and self-serving rationalizations.

Further, there is a need for *deconstructing the psychological interior* of the violent act for both parties, that is, a deconstruction of the moments leading up to a violent outburst and, not least, the moments of the aftermath. Deconstructing the violent act means expounding the action piece by piece, moment by moment. This process entails asking the same questions over and over about "how?", "when?", "where?", "how did you feel afterwards?", "didn't you ever consider another interpretation?", "if I had been in your place, I would have felt... how did you actually feel?", and "if you felt this way, how do you imagine what your wife felt?" Repetitious questions of this kind yield many varying descriptions of the violent act, thus bringing new meaning to the action.

In addition to the deconstruction of the psychological interior of the violent act, the *deconstruction of the man's logical frame of narrating* is called for. I will give an example of how this can be done. Let us consider the following conversation once again:

> **IP:** You see, in our heads there is a place with two poles. There has to be a certain distance between them. When you get angry, you get close to one of the poles. In my head, the poles are too close together, so that when I get angry, they crash into each other. I can see on you that you don't believe me, but it is in fact true. A doctor himself told me this. I think it was caused by a motorcycle accident I was in.
>
> **I:** How can you tell when this happens?
>
> **IP:** I simply get a total blackout. I get mad and then PANG, it crashes and I am not aware of anything for a long time. When I come to again, I have often done something violent. Hit Pia or trashed the apartment.
>
> **I:** Then it must be unbelievable luck that Pia is still alive.
>
> **IP:** What do you mean?
>
> **I:** I mean that when you get mad at her and it short-circuits in your head, your body takes on a life of its own and becomes violent. It is lucky that you haven't stuck the bread knife in her, or scissors, or hit her even worse than you have.
>
> **IP:** Are you crazy or something?!! Do you think that I could do such a thing? I would never be able to hurt her that bad! (Kjell I, joint interview)

In this conversation, the interviewer addresses the extreme manifestations of the logical frame of the narrative (e.g. a narrative of exculpation). The interviewer opposes the informant's account by questioning it to its extremes. The consequences of the suggested behavior are laid bare. The informant then abandons the originally used frame and replaces it with one that makes it possible for him to relate to himself as to a person of responsibility, in possession of full awareness and control capacity. In the wake of this altering of the frame, a new account of the violent act may get a chance to evolve.

When the informant couple, after the woman's revelation of morally unacceptable actions in the marriage, are invited to conversations about these sensitive topics, a context shift is established. The "marital monologue" has been replaced by a "dialogue of research". The significance of this shift could be presented in terms of sharing, of the researchers gaining access to previously closed situations within the family, and finally in terms of the elaboration of a new context to talk about what often is seen as "impossible to talk about". I would like to introduce the phrase "impossible conversation" to grasp the essence of the deconstructive work that took place in this shift of context. The underlying message from the researcher in this "conversation" is that personal responsibility could be something useful, not least of all in the process of gaining awareness and control of one's own individual life project – something that can be extremely difficult to gain for a person that entangles himself in the rhetoric patterns of exculpation.

By refraining from confronting the man's personality, and concentrating on challenging his ideas, another just as important message was implicated in the "impossible conversation". This mode of interaction meant challenging the basic pattern of dominance and subordination, the pattern that brought the status of the other person into question by means of the communication of worthlessness. It was replaced by the idea of a conversation along more symmetrical lines.

The new descriptions or narrative accounts for the man, that get a chance to evolve once the narrative of exculpation is abandoned, probably could be fitted around what was omitted in the previous story, namely, his own emotional experiences. By carefully separating all strands of the violent episode and by encouraging him to include feelings, a new story becomes possible, one including all steps of the actions taken – as well as including all the possible actions rejected. Such reinstatement of the narrator as a feeling, thinking, and acting subject in the text is essential. In the earlier accounts, the presence of the male narrator is missing; there it was possible for alcohol to batter, and the man never said a word about how sad and hurt he had been. A high degree of psychological pain and tension will be connected with this kind of deconstruction. The distress may be so pronounced that it sparks a genuine crisis (Stordeur, R. and Stille R. 1989), which will in turn place demands on the social worker's or psychotherapist's ability to soothe pain and provide psychological support.

If I had to identify a single significant factor in the maintenance of a marriage as a violent marriage, I would name the loss of a narrator in the account, that is, the lack of a man acting and taking responsibility for his actions. In the proposed narrative, the narrator claims his presence as an acting subject. The narrative probably could be fitted around another theme, located closely to his talk of his own emotional experiences, namely the question: "Do you want to remain a wife batterer?" In the case of a "no" answer, the new narratives of Hans and Mats can give an understanding of how such a narrative can be constructed. By confirming, not denying the occurrence of conflictive situations, by claiming, not disclaiming personal responsibility, a conscious strategy for managing without the use of violence can be constructed. This will in turn allow for the creation of a new marital social order to replace the rigid one of dominance and subordination.

A corresponding new description or narrative account for the woman probably could be fitted around her lack of commitment to her own safety in favor of accepting responsibility for her own as well as for her husband's actions throughout the violent episode. Questions that could lead the woman further towards a new account are questions about personal power, in contrast to the initial account which was built around the experience of powerlessness.

In therapeutic work with battered women, one often finds women of substance with strong opinions, who convey a sense of personal power, while at the same time expressing a feeling of overall helplessness (Goldner et al. 1990). The task here is then to change the terms of discourse to help the woman move from a victim position to a place where she becomes aware of herself as significant in the shaping of her own apprehensions. What she needs is a new context for her revised story. I will give an example of how this could be done.

A young woman sought me out for therapeutic consultation due to serious suicidal impulses following a battering. She described how she ruined her husband's life first by reporting his violence to the police and more recently by petitioning for a divorce. She had wanted to leave many times, but had always felt prohibited by his despair and pleas for her to stay. Furthermore, she did not want guilt feelings about having destroyed his life, especially since she had already had two people's lives on her conscience – her parents'. She was their only child, and she had caused them unending grief by her disastrous marriage. What they had dreamed of most of all was a daughter they could be proud of. This young woman was completely resigned and felt trapped.

"You must be a very powerful woman", I commented after hearing her account. "The lives of three people rest totally in your hands." Before the end of our session, this woman had worked herself into a veritable rage over the fact that she had accepted the power these people had given her. This had caused her to feel so paralyzed about her own life that she had been unable to imagine how to move ahead.

To know what we do and how we do it is basic and significant knowledge. That is, the ability to articulate for oneself the particular means one adopts for connecting with others. The discovery of personal power is of essential value for a woman, victimized by her husband's use of violence. This discovery will hopefully help her to establish boundaries and to define an absolute bottom-line in her new story.

Here I have discussed the deconstruction and construction work that I advocate in terms of constructing two new stories separately. The construction of a marriage excluding violence is thus a joint enterprise as well.

Recently, family therapy practice has widened its scope by bringing social problems such as battering and incest into the consulting room (Goldner et al. 1990). Previously, family therapy was profoundly mute on the subject of power and its unequal distribution in the family and in the society (Hare-Mustin 1978; Hare-Mustin 1987; Walters et al. 1988). In one way or another, family therapy practice has managed to omit power as an organizing principle of family life. Systems theory has been the primary way of observing and analyzing. Systems theory is so abstract that it may provide a seemingly coherent account of family phenomena while in fact omitting significant variables, such as power, gender, and the link between them. Since systems theory focuses entirely on the moves rather than on the players, who has the power over whom and with what regularity it is exercised never enters into the analysis. (Goodrich 1991). The change that has taken place is extremely valuable for the couples who want to continue living together.

The key to change in a violent marriage is to be found in the construction of a new story of the violent act, a story covering the transformation of the disclaimed action into an action for which the man is held responsible. Until then, the freedom to change the terms of the marital project will elude the parties – as will the freedom to leave the project.

References

Araldsen, T. and Clasen, A-C. (1983) *Kvinnemisshandling – om insnevring av handlingsalternativer.* (Woman battering – a curtailment of spheres of action) Oslo: University of Oslo, Research paper.

Austin, J.L. (1979) "A plea for Excuses". In *Philosophical Papers.* Oxford University Press.

Barker, D.L. (1978) "Regulation of Marriage". In Littlejohn, G. (ed.) *Power and State.* London: Croom Helm.

Bateson, G. (1958) *Naven.* Stanford: Stanford University Press.

Bergman, B. (1987) *Battered Wives. Why are they beaten and why do they stay?* Stockholm: Dissertation, Karolinska Institutet.

Berger, P.L and Kellner, H. (1970) "Marriage and the Construction of Reality". In Dreitzel, H.P. (ed.) *Recent Sociology no 2. Patterns of Communicative Behavior.* London: Macmillan Company.

Bernard, J. (1982) *The Future Marriage.* New Haven: Yale University Press.

Blumer, H. (1971) "Social Problems as Collective Behavior". *Social Problems*, 18, 298-306.

Bolin, E. (1989) "Kvinnojourernas roll och samhällets ansvar" (The role of women's shelters and the responsibility of society). In *Kvinnomisshandel* (Women battering). *JÄMFO rapport 14/89.* Stockholm: JÄMFO.

Breines, W. and Gordon, L. (1983) "The New Scholarship on Family Violence". *Journal of Women in Culture and Society,* 8, 490-531.

Brennies, D. (1988) "Language and Disputing". *Annual Review Anthropology*, 17, 221-37.

Brismar, B., Jansson, B. and Larsson, G. (1988) "Knappast kvinnoförakt att skildra svårt misshandlade kvinnors psykosociala bakgrund", (It is not contempt for battered women to describe their psychosocial background). *Läkartidningen*, 85, 17.

Bruner, J. (1990) *Acts of Meaning.* Cambridge, MA: Harvard University Press.

Burke, K. (1969) *A Grammar of Motives.* Los Angeles: University of California Press.

Butler, S. (1978) *Conspiracy of Silence.* San Francisco: Glide.

Christensen, E. (1984) *Vold ties ikke ihjel* (Silence does not kill violence). Copenhagen.

Christensen, E. (1990) "Börnekår. En undersögelse af omsorgssvigt i relation til börn og unge i familier med hustrumishandling" (A study of negligence in relation to children and young people in families with wife battering). *Nordisk Psykologi's series of monographs*, no. 31.

Cromwell, R.E. and Olsson, D.H. (1975) *Power in Families.* Beverly Hills, CA: Sage.

Cullberg, J. (1984) *Dynamisk Psykiatri* (Dynamic psychiatry). Stockholm: Natur och Kultur.

Denzin, N.K. (1978) *Sociological Methods. A Sourcebook.* New York: McGraw-Hill.

Dobash, E. and Dobash, R. (1979) *Violence Against Wives. A Case Against Patriarchy.* New York: The Free Press.

Elias, N. (1978) *The Civilizing Process: The History of Manners,* vol.I. Oxford: Blackwell.

Elman, R.A. and Eduards, M.L. (1991) "Unprotected by the Swedish Welfare State. A Survey of Battered Women and the Assistance They Received". *Womens Studies International Forum*, 14, 413-421.

Faulk, M. (1974) "Men who assault their wives". *Medical Science and Law*, 14, 180-183.

Finkelhor, D. (ed.) (1983) *The Dark Side of Families. Current Family Violence Research.* Beverly Hills, CA: Sage.

Finkelhor, D. et al. (1988) *Stopping Family Violence.* Newbury Park CA: Sage.

Foucault, M. (1981) *The History of Sexuality*, vol.I. London.

Gayford, J.J. (1979) "Battered Wives". In Gelles, R. and Cornell, C.P. (eds.) (1983) *International Perspectives on Family Violence.* Lexington: Lexington Books.

Gelles, R.J. (1974) *The Violent Home: A Study of Physical Aggression Between Husbands and Wives.* Beverly Hills: Sage.

Gelles, R.J. (1979) *Family Violence.* Beverly Hills: Sage.

Gelles, R.J. (1983) "An Exchange/Social Control Theory". In Gelles, R.J. and Straus, M. (1988) *Intimate Violence.* New York: Simon & Schuster.

Glaser, B.G. and Strauss, A.(1979) *The Discovery of Grounded Theory.* New York: Aldine.

Goffman, E. (1974) *Frame Analysis. An Essay on the Organization of Experience.* Cambridge, MA: Harvard University Press.

Goldberg, M. (1982) "The Dynamics of Marital Interaction and

Marital Conflict". *Psychiatric Clinics of North America*, 5, 449-467.

Goldner, V. (1985) "Feminism and Family Therapy". *Family Process*, 24, 31-47.

Goldner, V., Penn, P., Sheinberg, M. and Walker, G. (1990) "Love and Violence: Gender Paradoxes in Volatile Attachments". *Family Process*, 29, 343-365.

Gondolf, E.W. (1985) "Fighting for Control: A clinical assessment of men who batter". *Social Casework*, 66, 48-54.

Goodrich, T.J. (1991) "Women, Power, and Family Therapy". In Goodrich, T.J. (ed.) *Women and Power*. New York: W.W. Norton.

Hare-Mustin, R. (1978) "A Feminist Approach to Family Therapy". *Family Process*, 17, 181-194.

Hare-Mustin, R. (1987) "The Problem of Gender in Family Therapy Theory", *Family Process*, 26, 15-27.

Harré, R. and Secord, P.F. (1972) *The Explanation of Social Behaviour*. Oxford: Basil Blackwell.

Harré,R. (1979) *Social Being*. Oxford: Blackwell.

Harré, R. (1983) *Personal Being*. Oxford: Blackwell.

Haavind, H. (1984) "Love and Power in Marriage". In Holter, H. *Patriarchy in a Welfare Society*. Oslo:Universitetsforlaget, 136-167.

Haavind, H. (1985) "Förändringar i förhållandet mellan kvinnor och män" (Changes in the relationship between women and men). *Kvinnovetenskaplig tidskrift*, 3, 17-27.

Haavind, H. (1987) *Liten och Stor* (Small and Big). Oslo: Pax.

Hamberger, L.K. and Hastings, J.E. (1986) "Personality correlates of men who abuse their partners: A cross-validation study". *Journal of Family Violence*, 1, 323-343.

Hewitt, J.P. and Stokes, R. (1975) "Disclaimers". *American Sociological Review*, 40, 1-11.

Hoffman, L. (1981) *Foundations of Family Therapy*. New York: Basic Books.

Hotaling, G.T. and Sugarman, D.B. (1986) "An analysis of risk markers in husband to wife violence: The current state of knowledge". *Violence and Victims*, 1, 101-124.

Jaffe, P.G., Wolfe, D.A. and Wilson, S.K. (1990) *Children of Battered Women*. Newbury Park, CA: Sage.

Jackson, D. (1968) *The Mirages of Marriage*. New York: W.W. Norton.

Kaufman Kantor, G. and Straus, M. (1990) "The Drunken Bum Theory of Wife Beating". In Gelles, R. and Straus, M. (eds.) *Physical Violence in American Families*. New Brunswick, NJ: Transaction Publishers.

Kelly, L. (1988) *Surviving Sexual Violence.* Cambridge, UK: Polity Press.

Kohler Riessman, C. (1990) *Divorce Talk. Women and Men Make Sense of Personal Relationships.* New Brunswick and London: Rutger University Press.

Labov, W. (1982) "Speech Actions and Reactions in Personal Narrative". In Tannen, D. (ed.) *Analyzing Discourse: Text and Talk.* Washington, DC: Georgetown University Press, 219-247.

Leander, K. (1989) "Misshandlade kvinnors möte med rättsapparaten – kriminalpolitiska konsekvenser" (Battered women's encounter with the criminal justice system). In *Kvinnomisshandel, JÄMFO rapport 14/89.* Stockholm: JÄMFO.

Lukes, S. (1974) *Power: A Radical View.* London: Macmillan.

Lundgren, E. (1985) *I Herrens Vold* (Violence in the name of God). Österås: Cappelen.

Lundgren, E. (1988) "Innlegg ex auditorio ved Bo Bergmanns disputas over 'Battered Wives. Why Are They Beaten and Why Do They Stay?' ". (Extra opposition at the defence of Bo Bergmans thesis 'Battered Wives. Why Are...'). *Materialisten,* 1, 101-117.

Lundgren, E. (1989) "Våldets normaliseringsprocess" (The normalization process of violence). In *Kvinnomishandel, JÄMFO rapport nr. 14/89.* Stockholm: JÄMFO.

Lyman, S.M. and Scott, M.B. (1968) "Accounts". *American Sociological Review,* 46, 46-62.

Martin, D. (1976) *Battered Wives.* San Francisco: Glide

Martinsson, M. (1985) *Women and Appletrees.* New York: Feminist Press

Matthews, F. (1988) "The Utopia of Human Relations: The Conflict-Free Family in American Social Thought, 1930-1960". *Journal of the History of the Behavioral Sciences,* 24, 1988.

Mishler, E.G. (1991) *Research Interviewing. Context and Narrative.* Cambridge, MA: Harvard University Press,

Ong, W. (1982) *Orality and Literacy. The Technologizing of the Word.* London and New York: Methuen.

Pagelow, M.P. (1981) *Women Battering.* London: Sage.

Pateman, C. (1988) *The Sexual Contract.* Oxford: Polity Press.

Pizzey, E. (1974) *Scream Quietly or the Neigbours Will Hear.* London: Penguin Books.

Potter, J. and Wetherell, M. (1987) *Discourse and Social Psychology. Beyond Attitudes and Behaviour.* London: Sage.

Reed, D., Fischer, S., Kaufman Kantor, G. and Karales, K. (1983) *All They Can Do ... Police Response to Battered Women's Complaints.* Chicago, IL: Chicago Law Enforcement Study Group.

Russel, M. (1988) "Wife Assault Theory, Research and Treatment : A Literature Rewiew". *Journal of Family Violence*, 3, 193-208.

Sacks, E.A., Schegloff and Jefferson, G. (1974) "A simplest systematics for the organization of turn-taking in conversation". *Language*, 50, 696-735.

SCB (Statistics Sweden) (1991) *Year Book of Judicial Statistics.*

Sartre, J-P. (1968) *Search for a Method.* New York: Vintage Books.

Scarry, E. (1985) *The Body in Pain. The Making and Unmaking of the World.* Oxford: Oxford University Press.

Schafer, R. (1976) "Claimed and Disclaimed Action". In Schafer, R. *A New Language for Psychoanalysis.* New Haven and London: Yale University Press.

Schechter, S. (1982) *Women and Male Violence: The Visions and Struggles of the Battered Women's Movement.* Boston: South End.

Schulz, L. (1960) "The Wife Assaulter". *Journal of Social Therapy*, 6, 103-111.

Skjörten, K. (1986) *Når makt blir vold. En analyse av seksualisert vold i parforhold* (When power becomes violence). Oslo: Dissertation, University of Oslo.

Smith, D. (1991) "Writing Women's Experiences into Social Science". *Feminism and Psychology*, 1, 155-169.

Snell, J. R., Rosenwald, R. and Robey, A. (1964) "The Wifebeater's Wife. A Study of Family Interaction". *Archives of General Psychiatry*, 11, 107-113.

Stanko, E. (1985) *Intimate Intrusions.* London: Routledge and Kegan Paul.

Stone, L. (1990) *Road to Divorce. England 1530-1987.* Oxford: Oxford University Press.

Stets, J. (1990) "Verbal and Physical Aggression in Marriage". *Journal of Marriage and the Family*, 52, 501-514.

Stordeur, R. and Stille, R. (1989) *Ending Men's Violence Against Their Partners. On Road to Peace.* Newbury Park: Sage.

Straus, M.A., Gelles, R.J. and Steinmetz, S.K. (1980) *Behind Closed Doors. Violence in the American Family.* New York: Anchor Books.

Straus, M.A. and Gelles, R.J. (1990) *Physical Violence in American Families: Risk Factors and Adaptations to Violence in 8,145 Families.* New Brunswick: Transaction Publishers.

Studer, M. (1984) "Wife Beating as a Social Problem. The Process of Definition". *International Journal of Women's Studies*, 7, 412-422.

Walker, L. (1978) "Battered Women and Learned Helplessness". *Victmology*, 2, 525-534.

Walker, L. (1979) *The Battered Woman*. New York: Harper and Row.

Walters, M., Carter, B., Papp, P. and Silverstein, O. (1988) *The Invisible Web: Gender Patterns in Family Relationships*. New York: Guildford.

Wardell, L., Gillespie, D.C. and Leffler, A. (1983) "Science and Violence Against Women". In Finkelhor, D. (ed.) *The Dark Side of Families: Current Family Violence Research*. Beverly Hills CA: Sage.

Watzlavick, P., Bavelas, J.B. and Jackson, D. (1967) *Pragmatics of Human Communication. A Study of Interactional Patterns, Pathologies, and Paradoxes*. New York: W.W. Norton.

Wikström, P-O. (1987) *Våld* (Violence). Stockholm: Brottsförebyggande rådet.

Yllö, K. and Bograd, M. (1988) *Feminist Perspectives on Wife Abuse*. Newbury Park, CA: Sage.

Yllö, K. (1990) "Patriarchy and Violence Against Wives: The Impact of Structural and Normative Factors". In Straus, M.A. and Gelles, R.J. (eds.) *Physical Violence in American Families: Risk Factors and Adaptations to Violence in 8,145 Families*. New Brunswick: Transaction Books.

Young, M. and Wilmott, P. (1973) *The Symmetrical Family*. New York: Pantheon Books.

Swedish Official Documents

Stockholms Rådstufvurätt 1863, Brottsmålsprotocoll 3:dje afd. Stockholm: Stockholms Stadsarkiv. (District Court Reports 1863. From the Court Record Archives).

Justitierevisionen. Besvärs- och Ansökningsmål 1874, Jan 30 III: Rapport den 9 februari 1863. Stockholm: Riksarkivet. (Court Reports. From the Court Record Archives).